Everybody I Shot Is Dead

Photographs and Text by

Deborah Chesher

12930 Ventura Blvd. #674
Studio City, CA 91604
info@cheshercat.com
www.cheshercat.com

Library of Congress Cataloging-in-Publication Data available.

ISBN 10: 0-9796542-0-3

ISBN 13: 978-0-9796542-0-6

10 9 8 7 6 5 4 3 2 1

Book design by Deborah Chesher
Cover photo of Deborah Chesher by Peter Wood

Scans by SL Digital/Los Angeles www.sldigital.com
and Digital Fusion/Los Angeles www.digitalfusion.net

Printed in China by Palace Press International.

Limited and Open Edition Prints from this book are available at www.cheshercat.com

Contents

5   My Story

7   Dedications

14   Michael Bloomfield

22   John Hartford

24   Rory Gallagher

27   Paul Butterfield

33   Ronnie Barron

35   Back Door - Ron Aspery/Tony Hicks

40   Badfinger - Pete Ham/Tom Evans/Mike Gibbins

48   Frank Zappa

55   The Beach Boys - Dennis Wilson/Carl Wilson

66   Donny Hathaway

68   Grateful Dead - Jerry Garcia/Keith Godchaux

74   Tim Buckley

77   Darrell Anthony Sweet

80   Jimmy Witherspoon

82   Hollywood Fats

84   Mighty Joe Young

86   Albert Collins

88   John Lee Hooker

95   John Denver

98   Terry Kath

105   Maurice Gibb

112   T-Rex - Marc Bolan/Steve Currie

120   George Harrison

128   Billy Preston

130   Alex Harvey

135   Tammy Wynette

138   Papa John Creach

144   Downchild Blues Band - Jane Vasey/Tony Flaim

149   Peter Bardens

152   Waylon Jennings

158   Peter Wood

164   John Bonham

173   Stanley Turrentine

177   Hank Snow

180   Keith Knudsen

184   Rick Nelson

187   Lowell George

193   John Fahey

198   Malcolm Roberts

201   Gene Pitney

205   Harry Nilsson

208   Acknowledgments

My Story

Journal entry - Sunday, February 17, 1974

Someday I'm going to have to write memoirs on life working with rock'n'roll stars. I could write all sorts of stories about what they're really like. To this point I've worked with Jesse Winchester, Muddy Waters, Freddie King, John Lee Hooker, Willie Dixon, Tom Northcott, Bachman Turner Overdrive, Mike Bloomfield, Redbone, Jerry Lee Lewis, Commander Cody, Shawn Phillips, Rory Gallagher, Paul Butterfield., Emerson Lake & Palmer, Tim Buckley and snapped a few of John Hartford. After tonight I can add Van Morrison to the list.

Someday is here, although this isn't exactly the book I had in mind at the time. As a kid, I don't recall ever uttering the words "I want to be a photographer when I grow up" or "when I turn 18 I'm going to hang out with rock stars." Most would have guessed my future would have involved skiing or horses. When boys replaced sports, I thought about becoming an artist, but then decided to follow my brother to Toronto and attend Ryerson. I registered as an interior design student, figuring that was the best way to be an artist (kinda) and avoid the starving part. One month in, I hated it. But I loved hanging out with my big brother. He was studying hotel management but his passion was playing guitar and writing songs. It wasn't long before he found a pub where he could play at least once a week on open mic night. The Oxford Inn became our home away from home, and we soon befriended all the local players.

When I wasn't in class or at the Oxford Inn, I was loitering in the quad building looking for people to sketch. I loved to draw and it was a great way to meet guys. And one of the guys I met was a photography major. Around the same time, I was given a photography assignment in one of my interior design classes. My only photography experience had been with an instamatic camera, and I didn't even own one of those at the time. So, I asked my new friend if I could borrow his camera. He gave me a ten minute lesson on how to operate his Pentax SLR and off I went to shoot a roll of slide film. I had no clue what I was doing, but it was fun and somehow my first stab at real photography turned out really good pictures.

By Christmas, I had talked my dad into getting me a Pentax and immediately started shooting all the musicians that played at the Oxford Inn. I loved the music, I loved the musicians and I loved taking pictures, never imagining that it could actually be a job. In my mind, I was using my musician friends as guinea pigs to learn how to shoot so I could get an apprenticeship with a real photographer and work my way up. My old journals are filled with pages of serious thoughts on my work and my future, but nothing about being a rock'n'roll photographer. With my new found love affair with the camera, I barely managed to finish the year at school. And when summer rolled around, I chose to move back to Calgary, where I found an entry level design job at an ad agency, and took night classes to learn how to develop my own film.

When the agency job ended a couple of months in, a set of rich twin brothers asked me to run their start-up concert sound company that they planned to bankroll with their construction jobs. I knew nothing about concert sound and less about running a business, but what the hell? They both drove Alfa Romeo Spiders, and since I didn't have a car, they let me drive one of the Spiders to the office every day. What teenager could turn that down? My job consisted of fielding phone calls that didn't come in and calling established sound companies trying to figure out what equipment we needed to do the gigs that I didn't know how to get. I don't think the brothers knew much about concert sound or business either because we were out of business in a matter of months, so I decided to put on my traveling shoes and make another move.

I chose Vancouver because I had one connection, and within days of arriving I was shooting concerts. My first connection led to a second connection and the second to a third, and suddenly I found myself getting paid to take pictures of record company execs backstage with the artists so they could run the pictures in the music trade papers. It wasn't much money - at one point I wrote in my journal how excited I was to be getting a check from RCA totaling $125, which probably covered shooting and prints for two or three shows. But truth be told, I probably would have done it for free.

I had it really good in Vancouver. On average, there were two to three shows a week. It was a big enough venue to attract the top shows and small enough that we remained a tight-knit community of locals who all knew each other. I would generally have the barricaded space in front of the stage to myself, other than the occasional newspaper photographer who would show up for a few minutes to grab a shot for the nightly deadline. I stayed for the duration, and being the only girl,

l. to r. Some of my original slide boxes. My bulletin board in Vancouver with backstage passes. One of many self portraits. My '66 Chevy II.

I was always invited to the all-important after party for the band. We also had our share of off days for the bands, like the first time I shot Blue Oyster Cult and they were looking for something to do. I suggested they come to my house because we had a pool. I wrote out the directions, never expecting to see them again. Imagine my surprise when the entire band showed up for an afternoon of cannonballs. Like I said, I had it really good in Vancouver.

But being a "grass is always greener" kind of girl, I wanted to fulfill my longtime dream of living in California, so in November 1974 I gave myself a birthday present. A trip to Los Angeles to check out the landscape and figure out if I had a chance in hell of making the jump out of the little pond into the big ocean. I made the 1300 mile drive in 24 hours, stopping a couple of times to eat and once at a rest area for a two hour nap. I had no plan and no appointments set up, just an armful of 11x14 mounted prints and the faith that I'd have a great time and things would work out for the best. Some of the highlights as recorded in my journal: *I was here in time to talk to Barry Wood* (no idea who he is) *and he arranged for me to go to the press promo trip for Ringo...I'm staying at the Continental Hyatt House, L.A.'s rock'n'roll hotel. First thing I saw when I looked out the window was a gaudy ELP billboard. They're really into billboards here, and license plates with names on them...One of the first people I met here was Jimmy from N.Y. He sells displays to record companies. He's been my biggest help here. I couldn't afford to pay for more than two nights here so he's letting me stay in his room as he has two beds. It's pretty inconvenient but I'm saving $23/day. I also became friends with the Deep Purple roadies. Most of them are pretty nice guys.*

I zeroed in on managers of the bands I'd already shot, although I mostly ended up showing my pictures to the gatekeeper assistants. I didn't make much headway on the business side, but I had a great time and was dead set on making it back, permanently. By July 1975 I had $300 in my pocket and my '66 Chevy II packed up, but as I was about to drive away I got sick. Really sick. Turns out I had spinal meningitis. After two weeks in the hospital and another two recuperating, I finally made it to L.A. Not an easy move with no money, no connections and no green card. In hindsight... a crazy idea.

I shot whoever I could, whenever I could. I did publicity shots for musicians hoping to break in and took pictures of bands at the Troubadour, the Whiskey and the Roxy. My weapon of choice continued to be my Pentax Spotmatic II cameras. For color I used Ektachrome daylight, which at the time had an ISO of 160. I think I pushed it to 400, allowing me to shoot wide open at 1/60th of a second. Black and white was always Tri-X. The ISO was 400 which I pushed to 800 and probably shot wide open around 1/125th of a second. For me, shooting concerts was always about feel. I shot very little film, forcing myself to make every shot count. I would connect with the music, anticipate their moves and always try to capture their soul.

By the end of '75, I was disillusioned with shooting concerts - it wasn't as much fun in L.A. I had also come up with an idea to do a coffee table book of artwork done by musicians, so I shifted my priorities and followed that road. But I did manage to fulfill one other rock'n'roll dream. In 1976, I met a promoter/manager at Dukes (the coffee shop at the infamous Tropicana) which resulted in my first and only tour. I was the only girl with nineteen guys on a three-week bus tour of Eastern Canada in the dead of winter. The headliner was Canned Heat, still riding their Woodstock appearance and hit song, *Going Up The Country*. I will never forget Bob "The Bear" Hite (February 26, 1945 - April 6, 1981) greeting me every morning from the other side of a bottle of Jack Daniels as I boarded the bus. Somehow I am missing every frame I shot on that tour, but Canned Heat are within these pages in spirit and through their ties to many of the other musicians.

Everybody I Shot Is Dead is dedicated to all the musicians I shot and the following five friends, who directly influenced my work and helped me find my way. They are rock stars in their own right.

Dedication

Dave Zeffertt

June 29, 1938 - March 13, 2000

Pancreatic Cancer

Dave Zeffertt doing his thing at the Michael Bloomfield and Paul Butterfield sound checks.   *Vancouver - January 14, 1974 and February 9, 1974*

Dave Zeffertt and I met on the phone when I was running the sound company for the twins. Even though I had no idea what I was doing, Dave was generous with his time and indulged all of my uneducated questions about the business of sound. I think it was his passion for what he was doing that made him happy to share his knowledge. Dave was *the* guy at Kelly-Deyong Sound in Vancouver, the outfit that provided top notch sound for the groups that didn't tour with their own system. Which was a lot. And he was my one connection in Vancouver.

Dave was the first call I made when I rolled into town, and he immediately invited me to the next concert they were doing. He may have thought I was really into learning more about the sound business but when he extended the invite my response was, "Can I bring my camera?" He said, "Sure." And that was it. I shot my first 'real' concert and was hooked. I loved everything about it. The sound set-up, the arrival of the band, the sound check, hanging around waiting for the show to start, the concert, the encore, the backstage craziness, the tear-down, the party and especially taking the pictures. The rock'n'roll spell was cast and I was under it.

Since Dave was the big cheese who'd been around for a while and I was the unemployed kid without a clue, I'm sure he found me annoying at times, but he saw my passion and gave me an open invitation to shoot. And if a band manager asked what I was doing there, he'd say I was with the sound crew. After a month of concerts, I showed Dave my pictures. That's when he realized how serious I was, and sent me to meet Gary Switlo... the guy who knew everyone.

Dedication

Gary Switlo
September 30, 1946 - April 12, 1992
Complications of HIV

If you went to a concert or almost any other event in the Vancouver area between the late sixties and the eighties, you probably bought your ticket from Gary Switlo. Along with his business partner Tom Worrall, Gary owned and operated Concert Box Offices, which they eventually sold to Ticketmaster.

I remember the day I went to meet Gary. Their main location was on the first level of Woodward's department store. He had this 'all business' attitude that scared the hell out of me, partly because he was intimidating and also I knew he could make or break me. We didn't exactly hit it off instantly, but he did give me names and numbers of all the record company reps and let me use his name when I called. Eventually we became very good friends. We hung out, went sailing and had a wienie roast or two. He even let me drive his prized classic convertible Mustang.

Gary was the one person I stayed close to after I moved to Los Angeles. If I needed help or advice I could always call him. When I told him my idea for the *Starart* book he was immediately on board and my biggest supporter. I remember one time when I had a trip booked to London to work with Cat Stevens and the money to back the trip fell through at the last second. I called Gary, and after a short lecture he sent me a plane ticket to Vancouver and set up meetings with his financial people to see if they could help. Unfortunately, they couldn't help me because I had no collateral, but Gary stepped in and co-signed a loan for me. Of course he made me agree to make the monthly payments, which I did, but in the end I'm pretty sure he was the one that paid it off. He came to L.A. for the *Starart* opening party and had the biggest smile on his face. And he stayed a couple of extra days because I insisted on taking him on a climb to the top of the rocks at the Joshua Tree Monument Park.

I didn't see much of Gary for the next ten years. I finally gave him a call in 1990 when I was driving through Vancouver on my way home from a vacation. I met his wife and daughter and he insisted I stay a couple of days. We spent a few hours alone in his basement. He told me he was sick. We cried and laughed and talked about all the things we'd done. Then he went into a stash of memorabilia he had hidden away and pulled out this huge photo print of me with the *Starart* artists. He told me that out of all his rock'n'roll encounters and the thousands of bands he'd met and worked with, his most memorable experience was the opening party for my book. What a guy.

Dedication

Mark Wilson
Cancer

Mark Wilson with Black Oak Arkansas, Brownsville Station, Van Morrison, George Carlin, and Maria Muldaur

Mark Wilson just happened to stop by Concert Box Offices when I was meeting with Gary. Perfect timing. Mark was at the top of the list of people to call that Gary had given me. He was the rep for Warner Bros. and with Gary's in-person recommendation, gave me my first gig: Van Morrison at UBC on February 17, 1974. Mark and I bonded immediately because we had something in common - we were both nervous that I'd screw up the job. I remember Mark telling me to be backstage the second Van Morrison came off stage because he didn't know if he would pose for pictures and I had to be ready to catch whatever we could get. Van agreed to pose for a quick photo in his dressing room, then after the first shot he turned it into a mini photo shoot.

Out of all the record company reps I worked with, Mark was the coolest on the outside, and the most high strung on the inside. He was image conscious and wanted to make a good impression on the artists not only for the record company, but for himself. The more we worked together, the more he trusted me, and quickly realized I was an asset... bands never seemed to mind posing for a young chick with a camera.

There were times when bands refused in advance to do the backstage photos: Led Zeppelin comes to mind. But even though I wasn't needed by the record company, if it was a show I wanted to shoot, Mark always did his best to get me a pass. I really loved working with Mark. He kept me busy, he had great bands and always threw the best after-parties.

I only recently found out Mark had died after tracking down one of the other reps I worked for. I was told he died "a few years ago," possibly from cancer brought on by an aneurysm, or maybe it was the other way around. I was unsuccessful in my search for his birthdate and when he died, but at least I can honor him here and publicly thank him for all the shows. Without Mark Wilson, this book would have a lot less pages.

Dedication

Fabio Nicoli
May 9 (year unknown) - September, 1977
Alcohol Related

London - May 23, 1977

Friday, September 16, 1977 - I told him he was killing himself and his incredible talents but I don't know if I realized quite how literal I was being about it. After I got through telling him what I thought about his life, he just sorta looked at me and couldn't say anything. Like a little boy who knew what was happening but was too naive to change it. He talked to me about how hard his life was and how if he could save up enough money and pay off his debts, he would leave all the craziness and go off and live by himself in the country somewhere.

I was in London working with Cat Stevens on *Starart* and had called Fabio Nicoli in search of some of Stevens' originals and the original art for *Extraction*, an album cover Klaus Voormann had designed. Fabio was the art director at A&M Records in London. He was responsible for creating all the album covers, most notably Emerson, Lake and Palmer's *Brain Salad Surgery* and Supertramp's *Crime of the Century*. I met him on April 18, 1977 at 4pm...

Friday, April 29, 1977 6pm - Up to this point England has been good to me. I've somehow managed to fall into situations that have been very profitable for my work. Meeting Fabio has probably been the most advantageous thing that has happened to me. He has been a lot of help with my work, what with getting the Extraction thing together and taking care of getting my negs and transparencies made, at no charge yet. But he's also been somewhat of a thorn in my side. I guess I knew when I first walked into his office - it was a weird feeling - there was a hesitation the moment I saw him, almost a feeling of turning around and walking out - like I knew I was in for something on first contact. It was really strange. At first when he wanted me to come and stay I didn't want to have any part of it. I figured he was another one of those record company turkeys that likes to collect women. The first nite when we went over to Maureen and Isaac's he asked me to stay at his place but I had my doubts as to whether it would be such a good idea. I figured I needed his help for my book and I could just see him throwing me out on my ear after a couple of days and then I probably wouldn't be able to do any work with him.

I ended up moving to his flat after the place I was staying fell through. He took very good care of me, keeping me out of trouble even when he was getting into trouble. He opened up whole new worlds for me; the London party scene and the world of his best friend, Maureen Starkey.

Dedication

Maureen Starkey

August 4, 1946 - December 30, 1994
Leukemia

Maureen with her kids, Zak, Jason and Lee.   *Friar Park at Henley-on-Thames - May 23, 1977*

May 25, 1977 ...ended up spending a lot of time with Maureen, including staying at her and Isaac's flat a few odd nites. She is the only person I've met in a real long time that didn't irritate me even once. Not one thing she did ever bothered me. Anyway, on Monday afternoon she took me out to Friar Park to shoot the doorknobs. We picked up her kids and spent a couple of hours wandering around the gardens. What an incredible place that is. They've got all these caves that maze under the gardens. I took pictures of her and the kids. I hope they turn out nice 'cause I'd like to send her a couple. Afterwards, we went back to the flat and Fabio was there. We all just played around 'til the wee hours, taking snaps and trying to make a mold of an ashtray for me to give Klaus. It didn't work out but we had fun.

Two years later I was back in London for the book, and even though I'd barely spoken to Maureen since Fabio died... *Winkfield 3:15am Fri. 13 Apr 79 ...ended up going to Henley and then coming back here to visit Maureen. Had a nice afternoon and it ended up with her wanting my # of which I didn't know where I would be staying so she invited me to stay here. I have the flat that's separate from the house and am being treated great by all.* She put me up for three weeks at her beautiful country home. It was much quieter than the previous visit when after the day's work everyone would meet at Mo's Mayfair flat for drinks. Then it would be out to dinner and off to the infamous private club Tramp, where one time I suddenly looked up and realized, "oh, that's Pete Townsend who just sat down at our table for a drink and a chat." At Winkfield it was family time, and at one point even Ringo showed up to stay for a while. *Friday 20 April '79 ...went to an art store and went crazy on stuff for me and stuff for the kids and Ringo and Maureen...Went home excited to give the gifts, which all enjoyed and really got into. Was like an art school at the house and made me feel really good. Then the night turned into an all-nighter with watching videos and talking to Maureen. Seems I had an unusually large amount of time to spend with Maureen, but I'm certainly not complaining for that.*

Maureen had a huge heart and was fiercely loyal. She was quick to tell me that she hated the *Starart* cover. Even though it was Klaus borrowing from his own design of the Beatles *Revolver* cover, Maureen felt we were trying to profit off the Beatles fame. She was no longer a Beatle wife but she still had their backs. How could I not love and respect her?

The Musicians

Michael Bloomfield

July 28, 1943 - February 15, 1981
Overdose

Q.E. Theater, Vancouver - January 12, 1974

My rock & roll photos have been sitting in boxes for a lot of years. Color slides in plastic slide boxes. Black and white negatives in glassine sheets, long separated from the contact sheets I have yet to find. There were a few 11x14 mounted prints kicking around that I'd pull out if someone asked but that was about it. And I must have moved about twenty-five times since the photographs were taken so it's a wonder any of them have survived.

When I had the idea to do this book, I pulled out the boxes and picked five or so easily accessible shots to use for a book proposal and sent them out for scanning. That was May 2005. I had some interest from an agent but that fell through and I had to put the project on the back burner while I finished a couple of screenplays. Finally, in the third week of February '06, I bought a new scanner that would work with my OS10 and immediately dug into a stack of black and white negative sheets. All of the sheets were numbered and almost all of them were labeled with the name of the band.

I randomly grabbed a sheet from the middle of the stack – it was numbered but there was no name. I held it up to the light and instantly recognized one of the frames. I hadn't seen that picture since the day it was developed. My heart skipped a beat. It was the picture of Michael Bloomfield and me on a couch. The memories came flooding back. Somehow, I met Michael the day before his show. We had an instant connection. Not the rock & roll sexual attraction kind, more like recognizing a friend in someone. No need for pleasantries, we already knew each other, even though we hadn't met. I didn't even know he was Michael Bloomfield. I'd probably heard the *Super Session* album but I had no idea what he looked like. I'm guessing the connection we made was a result of some smart-ass comment from one or both of us. However it happened, we ended up in his rundown motel room that night. No, we weren't there for sex. We were just having too much fun together to stop for something as silly as sleep. Two kids who didn't want to get out of the sandbox. Also, Michael insisted I teach him how to take pictures, so I had no choice... he was leaving town straight from the show the following day.

You would think a guy like Michael, whose fingers navigated the neck of a guitar with artistic perfection, would take to the camera like a fish to water. Quite the opposite. I put my little Pentax Spotmatic II in Michael's talented hands and he turned into a complete klutz. He might as well have had ten thumbs. We were shooting Tri-X 400 film pushed to 800. The room was a little on the dark and dingy side so the shutter speed was a bit slow, around 1/30th of a second. Once we tackled the difficult task of focusing, I taught him how to brace himself and hold a deep breath to keep the camera steady. He was very serious about getting it right. It took a lot of practice, including both of us falling on the floor laughing before he could work up the nerve to push the shutter release button. He couldn't hold still. I think most of the pictures he took of me show how I failed him at portraiture – although he'd probably prefer I lie and say we were going for "artsy." He fared a little better with his still life work. He was really into that telephone. He kept saying, "One more of the telephone. I

Me by Michael Bloomfield

think I moved on that one. I can do it better." If nothing else, he was determined.

I wanted to take pictures of him but he hogged the camera. The only one I got was the couch shot. Of course, it was his idea. He had the curiosity of a three-year-old. That pointing thing they do while asking, "What's this?", then touching it without waiting for the answer. That's how Michael discovered the self-timer. I explained how it worked and he immediately wanted to try it out with a picture of us. He wanted us sitting on the couch. I set the camera on the telephone book and turned on the flash. Then focused, started the timer and jumped into the shot. It seemed like a long time passed before the camera snapped the picture.

The next day it was back to reality. Michael had to be at a sound check where his serious side came to the forefront and where my less than stellar pictures taken on no sleep somehow still managed to reflect the mood. I don't remember what songs he played that night but I know he was brilliant. I don't remember the name of the hotel, I just remember him. Michael, the person. As quickly as he came, he was gone. We didn't exchange phone numbers, no addresses. I don't know why. We just didn't. We had our goodbye hugs and said, "See ya'."

Over two years passed. I had been living in Los Angeles for a year and a half and was in the beginning stages of my *Starart* book, having already put together a mock-up of Commander Cody's art. A girlfriend called and wanted me to meet Al Kooper. I knew of him from the *Super Session* album he did with Michael and Stephen Stills. I also knew his reputation with the girls. Still, I was curious to meet Al, just to see if he was anything like Michael. Maybe he could put me in touch with him. I told my girlfriend I was interested but not if it was a date. In those days, if you agreed to dinner it was assumed that dessert would be naked. She promised me it wasn't a date and assured me he was cool.

She arranged for me to meet him at The Record Plant, the most famous recording studio in L.A. I had been there before to shoot pictures of an Australian band, Ayers Rock. It was different showing up there to meet Al. The way the receptionist looked down her nose at me when I said I was there to see Al Kooper made me feel like a groupie. Al came out to get me and my first thought was, what I have gotten myself into? I could immediately tell he was nothing like Michael Bloomfield. Like me, Michael was a jeans and tee shirt guy. Al was the big hair, sunglasses, tight pants, half-buttoned shirt type. I tried not to stare at his rock'n'roll 'how cool am I' attitude dripping from every pore.

Before I could open my mouth in protest, Al ushered me back to the private area of the recording studio for a tour of the infamous bedrooms. There were three of them, each sporting their own thematic décor. The most famous bedroom was the Rack Room, complete with a working rack bed and other s&m style accoutrement. I think one of the others had a animal theme and maybe the third had something on the soft side. What shocked me most was that one of them had an "Al Kooper" engraved brass plaque permanently mounted on the door. Now I knew I was in deep trouble. My mind raced. How was I going to worm my way out of this one? Well, at least his name wasn't on the door of the Rack Room. But how tacky was it that he brought me to his private bedroom at the very public recording studio within two minutes of meeting me?

Telephones by Michael Bloomfield

What kind of a girl did he think I was?

We sat on the bed. I tried to keep a conversation going. Anything to avoid physical contact. But I could feel the tension building. There would be no dinner. Al was going straight for the dessert. He tried to kiss me. I backed off. I had turned down Gene Simmons' tongue in the past; I certainly wasn't going to go for whatever Al Kooper had to offer in his boudoir. I was never very good in these situations. It was uncomfortable and humiliating. I was shy and didn't like confrontation. He didn't cross the line but he was very persistent in his mission to get in my pants. I did not give in. By the end of our non-date he was definitely pissed off at me, as if fucking him that night had been a given. I left feeling stupid and thought if I ever saw him again it would be too soon. I was very creeped out by the whole experience.

A few weeks later, Michael had a gig at the Troubadour, one of my favorite places. It was the kind of place I could go by myself and feel comfortable. People would hang at the bar out front and there was always someone I knew. And I was always allowed to take pictures. I arrived alone, camera in hand and found an empty table off the left side of the stage near the back. I was excited at the thought of seeing Michael again, but I was also very nervous. I didn't think he would remember me. Musicians meet tons of people on the road – why would he remember some silly young photographer he met over two years ago in Vancouver?

I didn't get the opportunity to see him before he went on stage so my only hope was trying to go backstage after the show. That gave me time to enjoy the music and work on my "Hi, remember me?" speech in the back of my mind. I was about to take out my camera and get ready to take some pictures when I caught sight of someone in my peripheral vision. I turned my head just enough to recognize the tall man with big hair sitting alone at a nearby table. Al Kooper! I swear he shot me an icy look that said, "What do you think you're doing here?" Fuck, what now? There he was – the living and breathing symbol of my personal humiliation – at the very table that stood between me and my access to the narrow staircase leading up to the Troubadour dressing room. I froze, hoping he didn't see me. Suddenly, I was uncomfortable sitting alone. I didn't move one muscle for the rest of the night. I kept my face shielded with my right hand, thinking about what I was going to do when Michael finished playing. Could I handle the additional humiliation if Michael didn't remember me in front of the guy who tried to make me feel like a loser because I wouldn't fuck him?

As the show ended, I made the decision. My desire to reconnect with Michael far outweighed the anguish of losing face. Okay, barely outweighed. I stood up and turned, ready to look Al in the eye. But he wasn't there. Relief. He must have left during the show. No way he was already upstairs. I waited a couple of minutes, then slowly climbed the stairs. And there he was...Al Kooper. I turned to leave but someone right behind me. I was trapped. I acknowledged Al with a polite nod. He ignored me. My heart was pounding.

What happened next was the last thing I expected. Michael opened the door. He looked right past Al and focused on me as if we were the only people there. His face lit up like a Christmas tree. He screamed, "Debby Chesher! Where

Television by Michael Bloomfield

have you been? I've been looking everywhere for you." A dumbfounded look washed over Al's face. I smiled at Al as Michael put his arm around my shoulder and scooped me into the dressing room. It was perfect. I was vindicated. Michael had given me back my dignity and didn't even know it.

We ditched the backstage gathering as soon as possible and went to my place. I was renting a room in a huge house in Hancock Park. We hung out in my room all night as if no time had passed. We talked a lot. He told me he booked a gig in Vancouver so he could see me and when I wasn't there he said he skipped out on the show. Left his guitars there and went home. I laughed. A sweet thing to say, but I wasn't buying it. Nobody would do something like that. We talked some more. He told me his hands hurt. I massaged them for at least an hour. Then he played his guitar. Sweet stuff, like *Great Dreams From Heaven*. Eventually I fell asleep. He played through the night.

The next morning I dropped him off somewhere. Maybe it was back at the Troubadour where he left his car. This time we traded numbers and addresses. He wanted me to call him the next time I was in the Bay Area to meet with Commander Cody. He told me he had a lot of artwork that he'd done and he wanted to be in my book. I called him a few months later and set a time to stop by his house. When I arrived he wasn't home. There was a note on the door for me to go in and look at the work he left for me and then to call him at another number. There was a scenic watercolor that was pretty good. And a drawing that was just okay. I looked around the house to see if he had his own stuff on the walls. The place was kind of a mess. Stacks of papers and magazines on the floor of his bedroom. Not much furniture. A couple of guitars. I called him and asked if he had anything else. He said no. I told him he couldn't be in my book. That may have been the last time we spoke. I moved. My number changed. And I was never very good at keeping in touch.

When the scan of the couch picture opened on my computer screen for the first time, I completely lost it. I remembered the picture exactly, except I'd forgotten the way Michael was holding my hands. We look like one of the old married couples sitting on the couch in *When Harry Met Sally,* even though at that point we knew each other for less than twelve hours. I finished the rest of the scans - the fire-eating shot is the only live photograph I have left - and wrote down a few thoughts, then pulled myself together and looked through another batch of negatives.

Me and Michael photographed by me and Michael.

The next sheet of negs I found was labeled "Blues Jam." It was a summer festival show with several blues greats but I hadn't notated the players. Figuring some of them had probably passed on by now, I googled "Blues Jam + Vancouver Coliseum" hoping there was a record of the show on somebody's web site. The first link that came up sent me to an article in the Chicago-Sun Times written by Jeff Johnson on February 12th, 2006. I opened the link. Turned out to be a completely unrelated article about Michael Bloomfield, marking the twenty-fifth anniversary of his death. That was weird. But then it got weirder. Toward the end of the article there was a quote from Michael's producer Norman Dayron, "...When he got frustrated, he would turn to his favorite thing -- watching the Johnny Carson show. One time he was booked to play for 3,000 people in Vancouver. The Carson show was on the same time, so he didn't go on. Michael walked out, left four guitars behind and checked into a motel that had a TV before flying home." Hmmm. His concert would have started at 8pm and Carson didn't come on until 11:30pm. Maybe he wanted me to know he was telling the truth. I googled the same thing a couple of hours later and again over the next few days but the link to the article never showed up again.

For those of you who don't know about Michael Bloomfield and his music, here are the broad strokes. He is often considered to be the greatest white blues guitarist. He was a rich Jewish kid who preferred to hang out in the blues clubs on the south side of Chicago. He made a name for himself playing with Paul Butterfield in the early sixties. He influenced Bob Dylan to go electric while playing on *Highway 61 Revisited*. After moving to San Francisco, he convinced Bill Graham to book the black bluesmen into the Fillmore. He started Electric Flag but quit after one album. He wasn't interested in being famous. He hated being exploited. He left the *Super Session* recording after one day so Al Kooper recorded the second side with Stephen Stills. In the seventies he recorded for smaller labels, including Takoma, started by guitarist John Fahey. He rarely breathed fire on stage and I believe I'm the only photographer who caught it on film. He was an insomniac. His drug and alcohol use has been widely reported, although I never saw him drink or take drugs. It is doubtful that he self-overdosed. The police found him dead in his car on the passenger side. There was no drug paraphernalia, no I.D. and no car keys.

If you've never heard him play, find his CDs and listen. Michael Bloomfield was an exceptional musician. He was also intelligent, mischievous, curious, a little crazy and a whole lot of sweetness. I was lucky to know him.

Michael with Roger "Jellyroll" Troy (also passed away) at the sound check.

John Hartford

December 30, 1937 – June 4, 2001
Non-Hodgkin's Lymphoma

Egress, Vancouver - February, 1974

You may not know John Hartford by name or recognize his face, but I bet you've heard his music. Born John Cowan Harford in New York City, he spent his childhood in St. Louis, Missouri, where he fell in love with music and the Mississippi River. By thirteen, John was playing the fiddle and banjo, and later formed his first band in high school.

John moved to Nashville in 1965. One year later, he was signed to a record contract with RCA by Chet Atkins, who urged John to add the 't' to his last name. His second album, released in 1967, featured a song he wrote after seeing the film *Doctor Zhivago.* The song, *Gentle On My Mind,* came to the attention of Glen Campbell and became one of his biggest hits. In 1968, the song won four Grammys®, two for Glen Campbell and two for John Hartford. It went on to become one of the most widely recorded country songs, affording John his financial freedom. After a temporary move to the West Coast, Hartford was a regular on the *Smothers Brothers Comedy Hour* and the *Glen Campbell Good Time Hour*.

John recorded seven albums for RCA, then switched to Warner Bros. Records in 1971 and released his groundbreaking bluegrass album, *Aereo-Plain*, followed by *Morning Bugle.* I'm not sure if he was signed to a label when I shot him in 1974. My February 17th journal entry mentions "and snapped a few of John Hartford" which probably means I just showed up on invitation from Dave Zeffertt or Gary Switlo. As I recall, he performed solo, alternating between guitar, banjo and fiddle, as well as foot-stomping on an amplified plywood board. This was the same technique that he used on his 1976 Grammy winning album *Mark Twang,* which featured his set of river-influenced original songs.

He released another twenty albums, including *Hartford and Hartford* in 1991 with his son Jamie. Despite an on-going struggle with non-hodgkin's lymphoma, John continued to write, record and tour. In addition to being a prolific musical talent, John Hartford was a licensed steamboat pilot, and published author with the children's book *Steamboat in a Cornfield.* He was also one of the narrators on Ken Burns' documentary *Baseball* in 1994.

In 2000, John performed on two songs for the hit movie *O Brother, Where Art Thou?; Indian War Whoop* and *I Am a Man of Constant Sorrow,* the only single from the soundtrack to chart. He also played on the subsequent *Down From the Mountain* tour and was immortalized in the concert film and DVD. His contribution to the *O Brother, Where Art Thou?* soundtrack resulted in his fourth and final Grammy when it won Best Compilation Soundtrack Album for a Motion Picture, Television or Other Visual Media in 2002. At the time of his death, John was working on a manuscript about the life and music of fiddler Ed Haley.

Rory Gallagher

March 2, 1948 - June 14, 1995
Liver Transplant Complications

Gardens, Vancouver - February 9, 1974

Rory Gallagher was a consummate blues and rock musician. Born in Ballyshannon, Ireland, Rory got his first guitar after seeing Elvis Presley on television. He began his professional music career in the early sixties, covering the hits of the day with showbands. In 1965 he turned one of those bands into an R'n'B band, playing concerts in Ireland and Spain. He formed the band Taste a year later and recorded four albums including *Live at Montreux* and *Live at the Isle of Wight,* where the band later broke up and Rory became a solo artist.

The seventies was Gallagher's most prolific decade, recording eight studio albums and two live albums. In 1972, Rory Gallagher unseated Eric Clapton as Melody Maker's Best Musician of the Year. He took every opportunity to guest with his heroes such as Muddy Waters and Jerry Lee Lewis on their respective *London Sessions,* and later with Albert Collins on *Jammin' With Albert.* His 1974 tour of Ireland was captured on film in an excellent documentary by Tony Palmer.

Rory toured relentlessly throughout his career, including more than twenty-five trips across the pond through the U.S. and Canada. He chose to forego a family life, and instead dedicated himself to his music and fans. He truly was a captivating performer. The concert I shot was another show courtesy of Dave Zeffertt, hence no backstage shots with a record guy. I wish I had taken more pictures and done a better job developing the film I did shoot but looking at the photos now, I think the extra grain reflects the feel of Rory's music. I was lucky enough to see Rory one more time, at the Bottom Line in November 1978. Unfortunately I went without my camera.

On January 10, 1995 Rory Gallagher collapsed on stage while performing in Rotterdam. That would be his last show. He was hospitalized in London in March for a liver transplant and passed away due to complications on June 14th.

Paul Butterfield

December 17, 1942 - May 4, 1987
Overdose

Gardens, Vancouver - February 9, 1974

Legendary harmonica player and Chicago native Paul Butterfield is best known as an innovator of Chicago-style electric blues. He met Elvin Bishop at the University of Chicago, where Bishop was a physics major. They started hanging out at the southside blues clubs and jamming with the black blues artist greats whenever they could. They joined forces with Sam Lay and Jerome Arnold from Howlin' Wolf's band and became the house band at Big John's. They were brought to the attention of record producer Paul Rothchild and, with the addition of Michael Bloomfield on lead guitar, he signed the band to Elektra Records. The first album was scrapped except for the Nick Gravenites song *Born In Chicago,* which ended up on a sampler and sold 200,000 copies.

After recording another album in New York (their first Elektra release, the now-classic *The Paul Butterfield Band*), they played the 1965 Newport Folk Festival, splitting the acoustic purist audience with their burning electric sound. Bob Dylan liked what he heard and asked Paul's band to back him later that night. The bold move garnered boos from the audience for Dylan but forever changed the face of the folk and blues movement.

The Paul Butterfield Blues Band began splintering after their highly acclaimed follow-up album *East-West*, with Bloomfield starting Electric Flag. By 1969, their success was on the decline but they were still popular enough to play Woodstock. Tired of touring, Paul dissolved the band and retreated to Woodstock. Fueled by the thriving musician's community, it wasn't long before Butter formed a new band that became known as Better Days.

I'd only been shooting legitimate concerts for a couple of months when the Paul Butterfield Better Days tour blew into town. I wasn't established with the record companies yet so this was yet another concert I shot on the invitation of Dave Zeffertt. Since I didn't have a ticket I showed up for the sound check to make sure I was in the building for the show. Sound checks also gave me a chance to get a feel for the band and their music. And more often than not I'd get to meet and talk to the band.

Paul Butterfield was an intimidating man. Downright scary by some accounts. Although he didn't seem to mind me hanging out on the stage while they were

setting up, I don't think Paul and I spoke more than a nod and a hello that day. I spent most of my time befriending his drummer, Chris Parker. Like me, Chris was young and we found a common ground in our passion for art and ended up spending the night at his hotel talking and taking pictures of each other. It wasn't until years later, on November 14, 1978 that Paul Butterfield and I really met. I was in New York working with Joni Mitchell on *Starart* and staying with my friend, D.J., who had a very cool music club called Trax with his friend and restaurateur, J.P.

N.Y. Nov 17/78 Fri. 9pm ...I had dinner at J.P.'s and then called D.J. to see what was happening. He told me to wait at J.P.'s 'cause Paul Butterfield had arrived and they would meet me there. Well I was getting very tired as I hadn't had any sleep but I somehow managed to hang in. We all partied around there 'til about 7am then ended up going to Barry's where Paul was staying. Had lots of good conversation etc... Paul was trying to convince me that he was an artist and should be in my book. I told him I only considered serious artists that had a body of work. We argued about that for a while and then engaged in a philosophical debate. It got pretty heated but I didn't back down. My sarcastic tongue was in fine form and I had no problem calling Paul on his bullshit. However, others did. I was told to "shut up" and "you don't argue with Paul Butterfield." Why? Because he was famous? I didn't care if he was famous. I was having a good time and I was pretty sure Paul and I were on the same wavelength. Seems my instincts were dead on. *...Paul kept saying I was a real good person which made me feel good, then he gave me one of his harmonicas. That blew my mind...I wanted to leave about 10am but D.J. didn't so we went to the store and discussed it. I just had these weird feelings that something was going to come down and I didn't want to be around to see it. Well, we stayed and sure enough around 3pm Barry found that [something] was missing. That was a drag. We stayed right through until Paul left for L.A.*

I loved Paul Butterfield. He was real.

Ronnie Barron

October 9, 1943 - March 20, 1997
Heart Failure

Bass player Rod Hicks, tech "Fastback", Ronnie Barron, Paul Butterfield, guitarist Amos Garrett　　　*Gardens, Vancouver - February 9, 1974*

Ronnie Barron began playing music in his hometown of Algiers in New Orleans. By his late teens he was playing the tourist clubs on Bourbon Street, where he created his Reverend Ether character, based on his made-up mythology about voodoo and gumbo. Mac Rebennack caught his act and hired Ronnie to tour with his band. When Ronnie left New Orleans for Los Angeles and a session gig with Sonny and Cher in 1965, he bestowed Reverend Ether on Mac and it became Dr. John The Night Tripper, the persona that made Rebennack famous.

After a number of years, Barron found his job as a session player unfulfilling and took an offer to play with Paul Butterfield's Better Days band. Ronnie's initial meeting with the band at Albert Grossman's house in Woodstock was rough, but he was quickly accepted when they realized his diversity on piano and his incredible vocal range. My friend and former Butterfield Better Days drummer Chris Parker describes Ronnie as a broad range thinker. Ronnie would take him aside and orate his philosophical theories on life (how "ontogeny recapitulates monogeny") and birds, which became the inspiration for Butterfield's song and album title, *It All Comes Back*.

In addition to five albums with Paul Butterfield, Ronnie recorded several solo LPs and played on many other artists' records including Dr. John, Ry Cooder, Eric Burdon, Tom Waits and Canned Heat. I ran into Ronnie many times after I moved to Los Angeles when he was playing with John Mayall and I was working with John on *Starart*. I shot lots of pictures of John's live shows during the late seventies but sadly I haven't found any that include Ronnie.

A few years before his death, Ronnie received a heart transplant. His family was told it was needed because of a heart infection possibly resulting from extensive dental work he may have done for his role in Steven Seagal's *Above The Law*.

Back Door

Ron Aspery   Tony Hicks

PNE Coliseum, Vancouver - February 14, 1974

Peter Thorup (guitar), Colin Hodgkinson (bass), Ron Aspery (sax, flute), Tony Hicks (drums), Mark Wilson (Warner Bros.)

Who are Back Door? I had no idea. I was there to shoot Emerson, Lake and Palmer. ELP was a huge band at the time and easily filled the 17,000-plus seats at the Coliseum. They had a big hit with *Lucky Man* and this tour was to promote their brilliant album *Brain Salad Surgery*. Back Door was their opening act. Like ELP, they were actually a trio playing jazz-rock with bass, drums and saxophones (Peter Thorup toured with them but was not part of the band).

Back Door were very popular at the Lion Inn pub on Blakey Ridge, Yorkshire but couldn't get a record deal. So they made their own record and sold it over the bar. Somehow it got in the hands of NME (New Musical Express) and received a rave review. That soon led to an offer to open for Chick Corea at Ronnie Scott's bar in London and from there they signed with Warner Brothers. After recording their second album in New York with Felix Papallardi producing, Warner Brothers sent them on tour as the opening act for their biggest acts of the time, including this one with Emerson, Lake and Palmer.

Ron Aspery started playing the sax at age twelve because he was fascinated with the way it looked. He met Colin Hodgkinson and, after a time playing in another band together, they formed Back Door in 1971. In addition to ELP, they

Ron Aspery

June 9, 1946 - December 10, 2003
Stroke

toured with Deep Purple and also did six weeks with J. Geils where Ron ended up sitting next to a blonde woman on every flight. Out of boredom he bought a magnetic chess board and the woman taught him to play. He didn't find out until after the tour that she was Peter Wolf's girlfriend, Faye Dunaway.

Tony Hicks started drumming and joining a band in school out of boredom. By sixteen he was working as a roadie for the band Ron Aspery was in and also sat in on drums. Then he went to Australia for a while and by the time he returned Back Door had already been together for a couple of years. Wanting to play with them, he offered their drummer 50p to take a night off and impressed Ron and Colin enough that they asked him to stay on permanently. It wasn't long before the band was signed to Warners and Tony found himself leaving his small flat in a limo with a first class ticket to New York for a recording session at Electric Ladyland. And from there it was on to playing sold-out baseball stadiums as an opening act. A bit overwhelming, to be sure. But they were really impressive on stage. They really held their own, even though they only took up a tiny portion

Tony Hicks

August 8, 1948 - August 12, 2006
Brain Hemorrhage

of the massive stage and were playing to the huge crowd waiting to see ELP and their "Welcome Back My Friends to the Show that Never Ends." There was a lot of joking around backstage while we were getting the 'band with the record guy' pictures. They didn't have a clue what they were supposed to do. Definitely out of their element. Wondering why anybody wanted to have a picture with them, much less publish it in a record trade paper.

After Back Door disbanded in 1976, Ron became a session player and film/TV composer. He contributed to scores on *The Spy Who Loved Me*, *The Oprah Winfrey Show*, *Friends*, *The Simpsons* and *Natural Born Killers*.

Tony Hicks went on to tour with many other bands, including playing a UK and European tour as part of Paul Butterfield's band along with Colin Hodgkinson. There was talk of them playing a U.S. tour with him, but it didn't pan out due to Paul's death. He also played for a time in the pits of the West End theater district. He spent the latter part of his life living and playing in Australia.

Back Door reunited twice, once in 1986 for a short UK tour and again in 2003 to record their final record, *Askin' The Way*, released by Cultural Foundation. The launch of the record brought them full circle with several shows back home at the Lion Inn on Blakey Ridge.

Badfinger

Pete Ham   Tom Evans   Mike Gibbins

 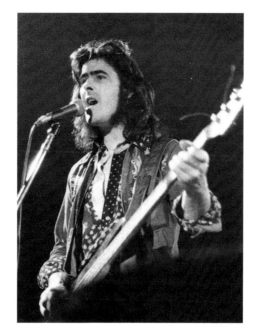 

Gardens, Vancouver - March 8, 1974

Badfinger had all the makings to become a storied success. The band was started by Pete Ham at Swansea, Wales in the early sixties. They went through several name changes until they became known as The Iveys and played in the local clubs. Drummer Mike Gibbins was recruited in 1965 and the following year the band relocated to London. Liverpool native Tom Evans was added in 1967.

While they played mostly covers on the London club circuit, the demos they put out to attract a record deal were original songs. One of those demos eventually landed in the hands of an Apple employee who passed the tapes on to The Beatles. They were finally signed to the label in 1968 and released the single *Maybe Tomorrow* to moderate success. At this point the band consisted of Pete Ham (guitar), Ron Griffiths (bass guitar), Tom Evans (guitar) and Mike Gibbins (drums).

The following year, Paul McCartney offered the band to cut a demo of his song *Come And Get It* for consideration to write additional songs for the Peter Sellers/Ringo Starr film *The Magic Christian*. It was accepted and they added two more songs, *Rock of All Ages* and their original composition *Carry On Till Tomorrow*, all produced by McCartney.

Prior to the release of *Come And Get It*, Griffiths was asked to leave the group. They changed the band's name to Badfinger and added guitarist/vocalist Joey Molland, switching Tom Evans to bass. Their second Apple album, *No Dice*, was released in 1970, charting at #28, with the single *No Matter What* hitting #8. But it was another song on this album that made a bigger splash. The Ham/Evans penned song *Without You* was covered by Harry Nilsson and remained #1 for four straight weeks in early 1972. It was also a hit and gold record for Mariah Carey in 1993.

Prior to their 1970 U.S. tour, Badfinger hired New York manager Stan Polley. He set up an American corporation for the band that put Polley in control of their earnings and salaries. Badfinger was well received in the States and their popularity continued to rise. They played on George Harrison's *All Things Must Pass*, added backing vocals on Ringo's *It Don't Come Easy* and played with Harrison on his *Concert For Bangladesh*. Badfinger's third and most successful album, *Straight Up*, gave them two hit singles, *Day After Day* and *Baby Blue*. While they were recording their fourth (and final) album *Ass*, for Apple, Stan Polley landed them a multi-million dollar recording contract with Warner Brothers. The release of *Ass* was held up due to legalities following their exit from Apple and didn't come out until late 1973, just months before their Warner Brothers album debut, *Badfinger*, which they were promoting on the tour I shot. Neither album performed well, but that was nothing compared to the unforeseen tragedies that would befall the band by the end of the year.

Happier times.
Joey Molland, Mark Wilson (Warner Bros.), Tom Evans, Pete Ham, Mike Gibbins

Pete Ham

April 27, 1947 - April 23, 1975
Suicide by Hanging

After their North American tour ended in early April, Badfinger were booked to record a new album at Caribou Ranch, a studio co-owned by Chicago manager Jimmy Guercio near Denver, Colorado. With family members in tow, the interpersonal relationships within the Badfinger family were tenuous at best. Pete Ham's friendship with roadie Ian "Fergie" Ferguson's wife, Anne, was perceived as the reason for their marriage break-up even though it was due to an affair on Fergie's part. There was also dissension within the band over management and money, as well as a growing rift between Pete Ham and Joey Molland because of Kathie Molland's involvement in the band's business dealings.

Months later, when the band was preparing for a UK Fall tour, Pete Ham walked out after hearing that Kathie Molland had been talking to various executives at Warner Brothers. The band quickly replaced Ham with keyboardist Bob Jackson, but Ham returned a few weeks later to rejoin the band, seemingly after a call from Warner Brothers that they would drop their interest in the band if Pete left. Then, shortly after the tour ended in late October, Joey Molland made good on his threat to leave the band.

Despite all the difficulties at Caribou and onward, the November '74 release of *Wish You Were Here* turned out to be one of Badfinger's most critically acclaimed albums. But unbeknownst to Pete, Tom and Mike at the time, Warner Brothers were positioning themselves to file suit over $100,000 they'd paid into a royalty trust account that had gone missing.

Tom Evans

June 5, 1947 - November 19, 1983
Suicide by Hanging

Meanwhile, Stan Polley threw them back in the studio, giving the remaining four members three weeks to record their next album. Even though the band had not been receiving their salary checks on a regular basis, they decided to go ahead with the rushed album, *Head First*.

Warner Brothers not only refused *Head First*, they pulled *Wish You Were Here* from the shelves in the early months of 1975. Stan Polley became more and more illusive, leaving the band nowhere to turn as they were still under contract with him. Unable to reach Polley in the coming months to resolve the legal and financial issues plaguing the band, Pete Ham, the most financially strapped member of the band, hung himself in the studio/garage of the new home he shared with Anne, who would soon give birth to their baby girl. In the postscript of a suicide note Pete stated, "Stan Polley is a soulless bastard. I will take him with me." After Pete Ham's death, Badfinger initially disbanded.

Tom Evans stepped back from the music scene for several months, until he joined a band called The Dodgers with Bob Jackson, but it took until 1977 for them to contract an album. Before it was finished their management company insisted on Evans being fired for his erratic behavior. A while later he got a call from Joey Molland to join a band he was with in L.A., a band that would get signed to Elektra and become known as Badfinger. During the recording of their album, they fired their drummer and brought Mike Gibbins, who had found success as a session player, including playing on Bonnie Tyler's #1 hit, *It's a Heartache*. Mike only lasted two sessions due to creative differences with the producer and returned to

Mike Gibbins

March 12, 1949 - October 4, 2005
Natural Causes in His Sleep

his session work in England. The album, *Airwaves*, was eventually finished and released to mixed reviews but the subsequent tour was well received. Before they could record another album the label dropped them and Evans headed back to England, later finding work writing jingles. But Joey coaxed him back to the States one more time for the recording of their final Badfinger album, *Say No More*, released in 1981.

During this time, all parties, including bandmembers and former management, were still fighting to gain access to the frozen Apple royalties, including the writer's share from the very successful *Without You*, written solely by Pete Ham and Tom Evans. In 1982 and 1983, both Joey Molland and Tom Evans toured the U.S. with their own Badfinger bands, the latter including Bob Jackson and Mike Gibbins. The tours consisted of mostly club dates and due to bad business decisions they were financially unsuccessful and resulted in another lawsuit by yet another nefarious manager. After a bitter telephone argument with Joey Molland over the *Without You* royalties, Tom Evans hanged himself from a tree in his garden.

Mike Gibbins got together with Molland and Jackson in 1984 for a short Badfinger tour. In the '90s he moved to Florida, where he continued playing and worked as a record producer. He released four solo albums; *A Place In Time,* in '98, *More Annoying Songs* in '00, *Archaelogy* in '02 and *In the Meantime* in '03. Mike died in his sleep at 56.

A comprehensive book, *Without You: The Tragic Story of Badfinger* by Dan Matovina, detailing the rise and fall of the band, was released in 2000.

Frank Zappa

December 21, 1940 - December 4, 1993
Prostate Cancer

Agridome, Vancouver - March 14, 1974

Is there anyone in the universe that hasn't heard of Frank Zappa? I doubt it. But I'm guessing most people don't really know who he was as a person. By his appearance alone, assumptions are made. Terms like freak, weirdo, hippie and druggie come to mind. Even though I was already a fan, I had plenty of misconceptions about Frank Zappa before I had the opportunity to meet him.

I first discovered Frank Zappa in 1970. Somebody at school had the album *Weasels Ripped My Flesh*. That was all it took for me to love Zappa. I didn't even have to hear it. The title and album cover was enough. I figured whoever thought to call their album *Weasels Ripped My Flesh* and was crazy enough to put that artwork on the front had to be a genius... and probably a freak. My admiration for Frank was cemented four years later when I heard *Don't Eat the Yellow Snow*, a song that summed up my childhood. I grew up in Calgary, Alberta where it snowed a lot in the winter. Since the time I could walk, I must have been told "don't eat the yellow snow" at least a million times.

Still, when it came time to shoot Frank Zappa in concert, I was a little nervous. Was he a freak? A weirdo? A druggie? I mean, his music was kind of whacked. Wouldn't he have to be all those things to come up with the stuff he wrote? And he looked kind of creepy, especially to a very young white-bread girl from Calgary. Yellow snow or not. All that long black hair and that odd moustache thing he had growing on his face. Not to mention his intense stare that emanated from pictures I'd seen. So, yeah, I was a little nervous. I didn't know what to expect.

I showed up early at the sound check to gauge the mood for the show and see if I could figure him out before I stuck my camera in his face. Zappa didn't seem scary at all. He was together. Focused on getting everything right, but seemingly good-natured. Without hesitation, I pulled out my Pentax and fired away.

When I photographed Frank backstage, I found him to be one of the most straight-forward down-to-Earth musicians I'd ever met. He was very sweet to me; personable, smart and dare I say normal? He had no problem speaking his mind and I got the impression that he had disdain for people who were unprepared and wasted his time. I was a little nervous when record rep Mark Wilson gave Frank a caricature drawn by a local artist. I thought it was risky to give a famous musician you don't know an artist's interpretation of their likeness, not to mention something of awkward size they'd have to cart around. I could tell Frank wasn't thrilled, but he still agreed to Mark's request for a photograph with the drawing to give to the artist.

A capacity crowd of five thousand die-hard fans welcomed Frank Zappa to Vancouver and they were with him through every note of every song. One of the greatest moments I witnessed at any concert was the frenzy Frank created when he picked up his film camera and turned it on the audience. The fans screamed with delight at being the subjects of a Frank Zappa movie.

Zappa crossed multiple genres with his music including classical, jazz, blues and rock. He was a composer, drummer, guitarist, record producer, technician, music editor, author, satirist, actor and filmmaker. And Frank was definitely not a weirdo, a freak, nor a druggie. He actively fought against censorship, testifying at a Congressional hearing in 1985 and appearing on CNN's *Crossfire* in 1986. Frank Zappa even planned to run for president of the United States. How great would that have been?

I love this photo and wanted to share it, despite the unknown smutch that is stuck to the negative. In the interest of authenticity, I chose not to retouch it.

The Beach Boys

Dennis Wilson   Carl Wilson

PNE Coliseum, Vancouver - December 11, 1974

From my earliest memories, I had a love affair with California, and synonymous with my love affair with California was my love for the Beach Boys. Most of my early childhood was spent in Alberta, Canada, nowhere near the sands of the Pacific Ocean. My closest connection to California was a photo album sandwiched in a crowded end table drawer in our living room. It was filled with 8 x 10 black & white pictures of a racehorse farm with beautiful Spanish house that my parents owned in Santa Barbara. I was only there in person a couple of times, but I was there thousands of times through those pictures. It's no wonder that my most memorable summer was the one I spent on the beach in Del Mar, California when I was nine years old. Wishing I was sixteen. Longing to be the Beach Boys' surfer girl.

Three years later I got to go to my first concert. Alone. Dropped off at the Stampede Corral with a couple of girlfriends. The opening act was Dino, Desi and Billy. I had a huge crush on Desi Arnaz, Jr. after having stayed a few doors down from his family that summer in Del Mar, and meeting him on the beach. Somehow we found out where they were staying and went to their hotel after the show. We didn't get close to them but I did see Desi's suitcase with the address tag, 1000 Roxbury Drive, Beverly Hills. I never did anything with the address but it stuck in my memory and after I moved to Los Angeles I learned that it was actually their home address. But I wasn't at that concert to see Dino, Desi and Billy as much as I was there to see the headliners, The Beach Boys. Wow. There they were... live... wearing their signature uniforms of the day. White pants and striped short-sleeved shirts. Clean-cut. Weaving their perfect harmonies on the songs that propelled my pre-teen fantasies.

A lot of things changed for me in the following years. I was older. Not so wide-eyed. Struggling to make it on my own. But some things hadn't changed at all. I still wanted to live in California and I still loved The Beach Boys, only this time I got to see them armed with my camera and a backstage pass. And not just once, but twice. The black & white photographs were shot March 17th and the color nine months later on December 11th.

Dennis Wilson

December 4, 1944 - December 28, 1983
Drowning

Dennis Wilson, Al Jardine, Carl Wilson, Mike Love   *PNE Coliseum, Vancouver - March 17, 1974*

Gone were the striped shirts. Their hair was longer. They had survived the sixties and seamlessly transitioned into being one of the biggest bands of the seventies, bringing their fans with them. It was a sold-out show at the Coliseum, over 17,000 strong. And my huge crush was now on Dennis Wilson. The middle son. The only Beach Boy that actually surfed. The bad boy. I'd seen him in the 1971 film *Two-Lane Blacktop*. Need I say more?

Dennis was originally given the drummer duties when The Beach Boys formed in 1961, because Carl was already on guitar and Brian was playing bass. As a vocalist, he had his first hit in '65 with *Do You Wanna Dance* and he began contributing his own songs to the group in the late sixties with *Little Bird* and *Be Still*, both on the *Friends* album. His solo work began in 1969 with the single *Sound of Free*, but he didn't release a solo album until the well-received *Pacific Ocean Blue* in 1976. He started a second solo effort, *Bamboo*, which he felt was much stronger, but it was never completed. Two songs from that album, *Baby Blue* and *Love Surrounds Me*, were used on The Beach Boys' 1979 album *L.A. (Light Album)*. Dennis was known for staying true to himself in his songs, writing mostly about love. Seems he couldn't get it right in real life as he was married five times, including twice to Karen Lamm, former wife of Chicago keyboardist Robert Lamm.

It has been purported that in 1968, after opening his home to a couple of female hitchhikers, he later returned to find Charles Manson in his living room. They became friends and even lived together for a time, prior to the horrific Tate/La Bianca murders. Dennis was known for his huge heart and would happily give away his possessions, but his excessive drug use and erratic behavior continually disrupted his career and relationships. However, it was still a shock when the news broke that Dennis Wilson had drowned while diving off a friend's boat in the chilly December waters at Marina Del Rey.

The color close-up of Dennis is one of my favorite photographs. Ironically, I would not have captured these pictures were it not for a hand injury he suffered in 1971 that kept him off the drums through 1974.

Carl Wilson

December 21, 1946 - February 6, 1998
Cancer

Dennis Wilson, Al Jardine, Carl Wilson, Mike Love   *PNE Coliseum, Vancouver - March 17, 1974*

Carl was the youngest of the Wilson brothers. He followed in brother Brian's musical footsteps, learning to play guitar at the age of twelve. Carl was only fifteen when the band launched and their first single *Surfin'* broke the top 100. By the mid-sixties, Carl took over leadership of The Beach Boys when Brian had to quit touring due to psychological problems. *God Only Knows,* from the influential *Pet Sounds* album, was the first song to really showcase Carl's vocal talents and charted at #39 in the U.S. and #2 in the UK. Carl also had the lead on the follow-up single, the phenomenal *Good Vibrations*, which hit #1 on both charts.

After the release of the chart-topping compilation album *Endless Summer* in 1979, Carl left The Beach Boys in frustration of their being perceived as a nostalgia band. He recorded two solo albums, *Carl Wilson* in '81 and *Youngblood* in '83, then rejoined the band to record *The Beach Boys*, their highest U.S. charting album since 1976, which included the Top 40 hit *Getcha Back*. The Beach Boys had their biggest chart comeback in 1998 with *Kokomo*, their first #1 hit single since *Good Vibrations* in 1966.

Carl was diagnosed with brain and lung cancer in 1997 and passed away the following year. An album he recorded with Chicago's Robert Lamm and Gerry Beckley of America, *Like A Brother*, was released posthumously in 2000 under the band name Beckley-Lamm-Wilson. Carl's angelic voice can also be heard performing backing vocals on Chicago's *Wishing You Were Here* and *Baby, What a Big Surprise,* as well as Elton John's *Don't Let the Sun Go Down on Me.*

Carl Wilson was credited with holding the group together over their nearly forty-year span, which was proven true upon his death when the band split into three separate touring groups.

Donny Hathaway

October 1, 1945 - January 13, 1979
Suicide

Oil Can Harry's, Vancouver - April 3, 1974

Donny Hathaway was born in Chicago but grew up in the projects of St. Louis, living with his grandmother. He started singing in church at the age of three and went on to be billed as *Donny Pitts, The Nation's Youngest Gospel Singer*. His talents on the piano earned him a full scholarship to Howard University in 1964. He left the school one year short of his degree to pursue his many professional job offers.

For the first two years of his career he worked behind the scenes as a songwriter and producer. He was a back-up singer for Curtis Mayfield and recorded the single *I Thank You Baby* with June Conquest for Mayfield's label. But it was his solo single *The Ghetto, Part 1* in 1969 that launched his career as a soul singer, followed by his first album *Everything Is Everything* in 1970.

Hathaway teamed with former Howard University classmate Roberta Flack to record a duet album that resulted in a 1972 Grammy award for Best Pop Vocal Performance By A Duo, Group Or Chorus for *Where Is The Love?* He also performed the theme song for the hit television series *Maude* and composed music for the movie *Come Back, Charleston Blue*. At the height of his success, Hathaway was plagued with depression and was hospitalized several times, causing a rift in his friendship with Roberta Flack.

I shot Donny during what is considered his 'period of relative obscurity' from 1973 until he reunited with Roberta Flack in 1978. There was nothing obscure about him, as he played several nights to a packed house with the full support of his record company. Donny's playing and singing was stellar and he couldn't have been nicer when it came to posing backstage. I didn't have a flash that night and I remember his patience as I struggled to find a spot to shoot in the dimly lit backstage area. Despite all our efforts, those pictures didn't turn out well enough to print.

His career was on the upswing when he reunited with Roberta Flack and recorded another hit single, *The Closer I Get to You*. They were in the midst of recording a second album when Donny fell fifteen stories from his room at New York's Essex House. Since there was no sign of a struggle and the window was removed and placed neatly on the bed, his death was ruled a suicide.

Grateful Dead

Jerry Garcia   Keith Godchaux

The Grateful Dead's impressive Wall of Sound.   *PNE Coliseum, Vancouver - May 17, 1974*

To supplement my income, I used to write articles for a local community newspaper on upcoming shows for about ten bucks a pop. I had titled my Grateful Dead article "The Dead Return" - if only I could make that come true - but the paper renamed it "Greatful Dead Return To Town," complete with the spelling error. In an effort to go back in time, here's what I wrote: *It's all happening Friday night at the Pacific Coliseum. The return of Jerry Garcia and the Grateful Dead. Since their last visit to Vancouver the band have apparently redesigned their already famous sound system. Instead of two speaker clusters on each side of the stage, their sound will surround you from four clusters set up around the building. No matter where you sit you will hear the finest quality sound available. Due to this change there will be anywhere from fifty to one hundred people traveling with the band.*

It all started in '64 when Ron "Pig Pen" McKernan met up with Jerry Garcia. Together with Bob Weir, they formed Mother McCree's Uptown Jug Champions. They played country music in the San Francisco area until the influence of the Beatles on the music scene convinced them to turn electric. With that decision, they added Phil Lesh on bass and Bill Kreutzmann on drums and became the Warlocks. The group then changed their name to the Grateful Dead in 1966. The Dead became totally dedicated to their music, playing all over California including many free concerts and festivals. They all lived together in a communal house which to some observers stood for a hippie drug cult. But to those who knew them, the Dead stood for freedom both in themselves and their music.

Mickey Hart (once a private detective) and Tom Constaten joined the Dead family prior to their fourth album "Anthem of the Sun." Constaten's stay with the Dead was brief as he left shortly after that album. The group then went economical with "Workingman's Dead," recording less musical breaks and more country style music. Keith and Donna Godchaux joined the Dead when they went on a tour of Europe in 1972. The triple album recorded from the tour was the last one for Pig Pen. He was found dead in his apartment on March 8, 1973. Since that time the Dead have recorded their twelfth album "Wake Of The Dead" on their own label, Grateful Dead Records. The Grateful Dead are probably best known by their FM followers for songs like "Truckin'," "Casey Jones," "Sugar Magnolia" and "Uncle John's Band."

Jerry Garcia

August 1, 1942 - August 9, 1995
Heart Attack

PNE Coliseum, Vancouver - May 17, 1974

During the early seventies, Garcia collaborated and did session work with musicians and bands outside of the Grateful Dead. He played pedal steel for the New Riders of the Purple Sage and produced their 1974 live album *Home, Home On The Road*. His pedal steel can also be heard on Crosby, Stills, Nash and Young's *Teach Your Children* and folk duo Brewer & Shipley's album *Tarkio*, which also included Paul Butterfield on electric guitar.

By the end of the seventies, drug use amongst members of the band damaged the chemistry that had made their past live performances great. Garcia's drug use continued to increase and in 1986 he fell into a diabetic coma that lasted several days and nearly cost him his life. After another drug relapse in '89, Jerry worked hard at living a healthier life; eating well, exercising and spending his off time drawing and painting in his art studio. But by 1995, his health was on the decline again and while seeking treatment at a rehabilitation center, he suffered a fatal heart attack.

Keith Godchaux

July 19, 1948 - July 21 4, 1980
Car Accident

PNE Coliseum, Vancouver   May 17, 1974

It was good timing that landed Keith Godchaux in the Grateful Dead. His wife, Donna, cornered Jerry Garcia at a show to introduce her keyboard playing husband just when the band was looking for someone to replace the ailing Ron "Pigpen" McKernan. Prior to the Dead, Keith played keyboards for Dave Mason.

When the Dead went on hiatus in '75, Keith and Donna Godchaux recorded *Keith and Donna*, which Garcia played on. Keith and Donna were also members of the Jerry Garcia Band from 1976-1978, and Keith wrote *Six Feet of Snow* with Lowell George of Little Feat (George produced the Grateful Dead album *Shakedown Street*). The rigors of the road finally caught up with Godchaux in 1979, and it was decided that he and Donna would leave the band. The Godchauxes went on to form The Heart of Gold Band, but Keith was killed in a car accident shortly thereafter.

The Grateful Dead formally disbanded in 1995, upon the death of Jerry Garcia. In their thirty years together, the Grateful Dead played over 2300 live concerts.

Tim Buckley

February 14, 1947 - June 29, 1975
Heroin Overdose

Egress, Vancouver - June 11, 1974

It seems like every time I turned around Tim Buckley was playing Vancouver. This is part of an article I wrote about the show where most of these photographs were taken: *Tim Buckley will appear June 11th to 15th at the Egress. He's one of the most exciting performers you'll see on stage and his music is dynamite. The incredible range in his voice and the powerful music expose lyrics which are raw and to the point. Tim Buckley has played in Vancouver twice this year, at the Egress and the Gardens. If you missed him then, be sure to catch the show this time.*

I met Tim Buckley at the tail end of his career and life. I had no idea of the rocky road he traveled. The struggles he had with the business, his financial ups and downs, nor the fans he alienated along the way with his ever-changing styles from folk to blues to jazz and his experimentations with his wide vocal range. Tim moved from New York to Anaheim, California when he was ten. He landed his first recording deal with Elektra in 1966, after he was introduced to Frank Zappa's manager, Herb Cohen. He recorded nine albums over his short career, with *Happy Sad* charting the highest at #81.

The Tim Buckley I knew was a bright, complex guy and a very talented way-too-charismatic smart-ass. I have vivid memories of standing in a cramped backstage area with Tim and his band before they took the stage. I knew him and the band well enough to feel comfortable joining in on the pre-show banter that flew back and forth. I must have made some crack about why they played Vancouver so much. I remember Buckley turned to me and quipped something to the effect of "you'd be a really hot chick if you dropped a few pounds." True or not, Tim could get away with stuff like that because he said it through the most charming boyish grin you've ever seen. So charming, I couldn't help myself from replying in all seriousness, "Thanks, Tim." Some say Buckley sold out and was just going through the motions in his final years but every time I saw Tim play he gave me goosebumps. Especially when he sang Fred Neil's *Dolphins*. You can't manufacture that.

I was looking forward to seeing Tim play when I moved to L.A. but he died of a heroin overdose (snorted, not shot) a month before I arrived. I looked up his guitar player, Joe Falsia, and we spent many an hour lamenting the loss of Tim Buckley. Joe had produced Tim's last studio album *Look at the Fool* and was planning a posthumous release and I was hoping to do the cover.

In 1997, tragedy also struck Tim's son, musician Jeff Buckley, when he accidentally drowned in Wolf River Harbor at the age of 30.

Darrell Anthony Sweet

May 16, 1947 - April 30, 1999
Heart Attack

Agridome, Vancouver - March 14, 1974

Darrell Anthony Sweet was one of the founding members of the hard rock band *Nazareth*. Prior to 1968, they were a ballroom band in Dunfermline Scotland known as The Shadetts and forced to play UK Top 30 covers. All four members of *Nazareth* were also married with families, not the typical profile of an up and coming rock'n'roll band. But that didn't stop them from leaving Scotland for London in pursuit of their dream.

After two albums and touring with Deep Purple, the band released *Razamanaz* in 1973 and found success with the single *Broken Down Angel*. I shot them when they toured for their fourth album *Loud 'N' Proud*. Their hard rock version of the Joni Mitchell ballad *This Flight Tonight* was a big hit in Canada at the time, and established the band as a fan favorite. Their biggest hit came in 1975 with another cover, *Love Hurts*. The band went on to become known as one of the hardest working touring bands in rock'n'roll.

Sweet's drumming skills were certainly a driving force behind the band's huge success. After being together for over thirty years, the surviving members of Nazareth were devastated by the sudden and tragic death of Darrell Sweet. The band had just arrived at the New Albany Amphitheater in Indiana to launch the second leg of their *Boogaloo* tour when Darrell fell ill and suffered a massive heart attack.

Jimmy Witherspoon

August 8, 1920 - September 18, 1997
Natural Causes in His Sleep

Super Blues Jam, Gardens, Vancouver - June 23, 1974

Legendary blues and jazz singer Jimmy "Spoon" Witherspoon was born into a musical family in Gurdon, Arkansas but didn't pursue a music career until after he served as a merchant marine in WWII. He had his first hit record in 1949 with *Ain't Nobody's Business*, and went on to record over two hundred albums during his fifty-year career. A performance at the Monterey Jazz Festival in 1959 cemented his reputation as one of the greats.

Spoon was known for working with young musicians and helping them launch their careers. In 1970 he brought phenom guitarist Robben Ford (who played with George Harrison when I shot him) to the attention of his manager, then moved him to Los Angeles and took him on tour. They played together again at a small Los Angeles blues club toward the end of Spoon's career, which culminated in the Grammy nominated album *Live At The Mint*.

Jimmy Witherspoon continued his tradition of working with the young guys for the show I shot. It was an all-day blues event so there was lots of great music and lots of hanging around. I wound up spending some time with Spoon's very young (maybe seventeen or eighteen) harp player. He told me that Spoon heard him play one day and invited him on the road. The other young one he had in Vancouver was twenty-year-old blues guitarist Hollywood Fats, seen in the picture above and honored next.

Hollywood Fats

March 17, 1954 - December 8, 1986
Cardiac Arrest/Heroin

Super Blues Jam, Gardens, Vancouver - June 23, 1974

Hollywood Fats is probably the best blues guitarist who has remained virtually unknown in life and in death. He was born Michael Mann in the Los Angeles area and began playing guitar at age ten. Fats found his love of the blues by the time he was thirteen. His mother would drive him to South Central L.A. to hear blues greats like Junior Wells and Buddy Guy, who gave him the nickname "Hollywood Fats."

Much like Michael Bloomfield, Fats was not intimidated to take the stage and jam with his blues heroes. It paid off. Soon he was touring with the likes of John Lee Hooker, Albert King, Jimmy Witherspoon and Muddy Waters. These photos were taken at Blues Jam when Fats was barely twenty years old and playing with the great Jimmy Witherspoon. The all-day event also included Albert Collins, Mighty Joe Young and Taj Mahal.

Also in 1974, Fats joined forces with Al Blake and Fred Kaplan to form the Hollywood Fats Band, and later added Larry Taylor of Canned Heat fame. The band recorded one album in 1979. It was considered a blues milestone but only managed to garner a small cult following. The band broke up and Fats went on to play with the James Harman Band, then replaced Dave Alvin in the Blasters in 1986. Still, he longed to play the blues. Towards the end of the year the Hollywood Fats Band was reunited.

But the dream wouldn't last long. After their first gig at a Christmas party for a Los Angeles blues society, Fats went out to celebrate and his life ended with a fatal heart attack due to heroin use. Hollywood Fats was only thirty-two and far short of seeing his talents recognized. The Hollywood Fats Band album was reissued in 1993 under the title *Rock This House*. In 2006, Delta Groove released previously unissued live recordings called *Larger Than Life*.

Albert Collins

October 1, 1932 - November 24, 1993
Cancer

Super Blues Jam, Gardens, Vancouver - June 23, 1974

Texas-born Albert Collins was known as the "Master of the Telecaster" and "The Ice Man" for his unique playing style on the guitar and because, like his music, he was cool. So cool, in fact, that he referenced the lower end of the thermometer in many of his song and album titles. His first single, released in 1959 was called *Freeze*. Then there was *Defrost*, *Frosty*, *Thaw-out* and *Sno-cone*. His chilly album titles included *Ice Pickin'*, *Frostbite*, *Frozen Alive*, *Cold Snap* and *Iceman*. And he eventually called his band "The Icebreakers." Collins was also one of the most colorful blues performers of his time, a great showman who knew how to connect with his audience. He used a guitar cord that could stretch hundreds of feet so he could walk through the crowd. On one occasion he was known to have walked through the audience, out of the building and across the street where he ordered a pizza without missing a note.

On the urging of Bob Hite - yes, the same Bob Hite from Canned Heat that I toured with for three weeks and don't have one picture to show for it - Albert Collins moved to Los Angeles in 1968 and was signed to Imperial Records, where he recorded three albums. It is purported that Collins quit playing altogether when he was dropped from Imperial in the early seventies and took a job in construction until he was signed by Alligator Records in 1977. There was a break in his recordings between 1971 and 1978, but he was definitely playing live at the Super Blues Jam in '74.

Albert Collins is credited with influencing the next generation of blues guitarists, including Robert Cray and Stevie Ray Vaughan. Collins frequently played in Austin, Texas and appeared on *Austin City Limits* in 1991. And he can be seen playing himself in the film *Adventures In Babysitting*, as well as on his own concert DVDs. The Ice Man passed away at his home in Las Vegas within four months of being diagnosed with liver cancer

Mighty Joe Young

September 23, 1927 - March 24, 1999
Spinal Surgery Complications

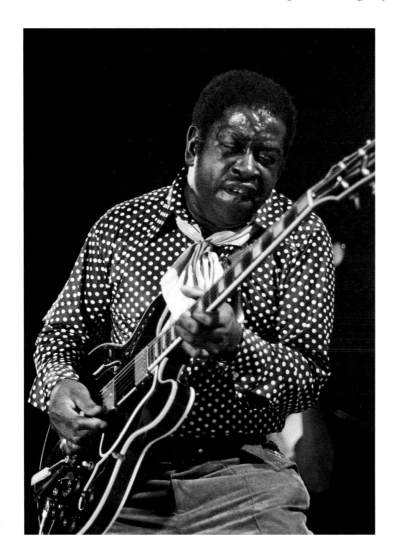

Super Blues Jam, Gardens, Vancouver - June 23, 1974

Mighty Joe Young was born in Shreveport, Louisiana, but grew up in Milwaukee and Los Angeles, where he became an amateur boxer. In the early fifties, he turned to a career in music. He moved to Chicago in the mid-fifties and began playing clubs with Joe Little and his Heartbreakers, Jimmy Rogers and Otis Rush. During this period he also recorded several singles for various companies and earned the addition of "Mighty" to his name because of his boxer's physique.

Young is known for being one of the first to bring blues music to the predominately white audiences in the North Side clubs of Chicago. He played regularly at the Wise Fools Pub and was well known on the college and festival circuits. In 1986, he decided to finance his own record but was sidetracked by having to undergo surgery for a pinched nerve in his neck. Complications caused him to lose feeling in his fingers, making it hard for him to play the guitar. He finally finished the album, *Mighty Man*, but it took him ten years.

In February 1999, he went in for spinal surgery, hoping to regain his ability to play the guitar. Again, there were complications that kept him in the hospital until he passed away on March 24th.

The Blues Jam was one of those days that has stayed with me. It was low-key and relaxed, but filled with feeling. The amazing musicians were there because they loved to play - the way it's supposed to be. It was the kind of day that makes you remember everything, from the music to the people to the scent in the air.

John Lee Hooker

August 22, 1920 - June 21, 2001
Natural Causes in His Sleep

Cave, Vancouver - July, 1974

Shooting blues greats like John Lee Hooker was a completely different experience. They had a vibe unto themselves. Even though I was still a kid and my musical tastes were in their infancy, when I met John Lee Hooker and saw him play, I knew I was in the presence of greatness. Nobody had to tell me. I could feel it. He had no airs about him. There was never an entourage. Just a quiet, yet fascinating man.

John Lee Hooker was the first concert I shot when I moved to Vancouver in December 1973. I have since lost those negatives. I am also missing the negatives of his show I shot at the Jubilee Auditorium in Calgary. I'm still kicking myself over that one because the roll had one of the best pictures I have ever taken. I was wandering around backstage before the show and caught a glimpse of John Lee Hooker in an open dressing room. The kind of dressing room with long counter tops and large make-up mirrors framed by big light bulbs. Mr. Hooker was alone, sitting in front of the mirror. There were cards laid out on the counter. He was playing a game of solitaire. I quietly entered the room and took a picture of him from the back with the reflection of his face and the cards in the mirror. He glanced up for a second, looked at my reflection, then went back to his cards. I asked if I was disturbing him. He said no and told me I could take as many pictures as I liked. I took six or seven more and then let him be.

John Lee was born in Mississippi, where his father was a preacher and only allowed him to listen to gospel music. After his parents divorced, his mother married blues singer Will Moore, who John Lee credited as his main blues influence. He was home schooled but remained illiterate. He had no interest in learning to read or write, believing books would get in the way of his music. He ran away from home at fourteen and landed in Memphis. He was found and returned home, then ran away again. It was the last time he saw his mother and stepfather. After working odd jobs and playing at house parties

John Lee Hooker, Uwe Schnack (RCA Records), Ed Preston (President RCA Canada), and below, John Ford (my client at RCA)

in Memphis, he eventually made his way to Detroit where his music career took off. In 1948, his first single *Boogie Chillen* sold a million copies, although Hooker received no writing royalties. He recorded over one hundred songs during the fifties and early sixties, including the hits *I'm In The Mood, Crawling Kingsnake* and *Boom Boom*. He reached superstar status in the sixties after the young British blues artists - John Mayall, The Yardbirds and The Animals - introduced Hooker's music to a younger audience.

He moved to Los Angeles in the early seventies and began recording with rock musicians Van Morrison and Canned Heat. Hooker won four Grammys, including a Lifetime Achievement Award in 2000, and was inducted into the Blues Hall of Fame in 1980, the Rock and Roll Hall of Fame in 1991 and received a star on the Hollywood Walk of Fame in '97. John Lee Hooker continued to tour and record until his death in 2001, leaving a rich legacy of music for future generations.

John Denver

December 31, 1943 - October 12, 1997
Plane Crash

PNE Coliseum, Vancouver - July, 1974

I really looked forward to meeting John Denver. I related to his music, especially *Rocky Mountain High* since I grew up near the Rocky Mountains and spent much of my childhood skiing them. He also reminded me of my brother, John, who plays guitar and is a singer/songwriter. They had the same haircut and wore similar glasses. And they both loved to fly airplanes. The biggest difference? I don't think my brother could sell out the 17,000 seats at the Coliseum in Vancouver.

John Denver was born Henry John Deutschendorf, Jr. in Roswell, New Mexico but moved frequently growing up because his dad was an Air Force officer and flight instructor. He learned to play guitar on a 1910 acoustic Gibson that he inherited from his grandmother. He played local clubs while attending Texas Tech University, but dropped out in 1964 to pursue a music career in Los Angeles. He changed his last name to Denver, after the city in Colorado, and played the underground folk clubs until '65 when he beat out over 200 musicians for the job of lead singer for the popular Mitchell Trio, replacing Chad Mitchell. Denver wrote and recorded *Leaving On A Jet Plane* while with the trio, which became the only #1 hit for Peter, Paul & Mary.

John broke out as a solo artist in the early seventies with a string of hits including *Annie's Song, Rocky Mountain High, Thank God I'm a Country Boy, Sunshine On My Shoulders* and *Take Me Home, Country Roads*. He made appearances on *The Muppets* and starred in the 1977 film *Oh, God!* with George Burns. He was also a dedicated environmentalist and political activist. He founded *The Hunger Project* with Werner Erhard and was appointed to the President's Commission on World Hunger by President Jimmy Carter. He testified with Frank Zappa against censorship at a Congressional hearing in 1985 and performed benefit concerts in Russia after the Chernobyl accident in '92.

I didn't get a lot of live shots at his concert. The stage was set lower than usual and they had reserved seats on the floor level instead. The audience actually sat in chairs and politely listened to the show, making it impossible for me to shoot from the front of the stage. I did end up with lots of backstage shots after I was barraged by the unusual number of fans and friends they let backstage, all wanting their picture taken with Denver. To my surprise, John accommodated every single request with a big smile on his face. And he was genuinely appreciative when he was awarded a gold record from RCA Canada.

John Denver was killed flying an experimental Long-EZ two-seater plane off the California coast. He was cremated with his grandmother's guitar and his ashes were scattered over the Colorado Rocky Mountains.

John Denver with Ed Preston (RCA Canada president), Uwe Schnack (RCA Records), and John Ford (my client at RCA).

Terry Kath

January 31, 1946 - January 23, 1978
Accidental Gunshot to the Head

PNE Coliseum, Vancouver - July 17, 1974

An excerpt from the article I wrote about Chicago the week before they played the Coliseum: *Chicago is a one-of-a-kind band in several categories. They are one of the few groups that still consists of the original members; after seven albums yet. They are also one of the few groups that can play a city year after year and always sell out. What is it that Chicago has? Maybe it's the seven fine musicians that make up the group. Or maybe it's the consistently good rock-jazz music they put out that keeps the crowds coming back for more. At any rate, by the time you read this you'll be lucky if there's a ticket left.*

Chicago started out in Chicago as a revolutionary bar and dance band under the name of the Big Thing. Their rock-jazz sounds are a result of Terry Kath on guitar, Peter Cetera on bass, Robert Lamm on keyboards, Lee Loghnane on trumpet, Jim Pankow on trombone, Walter Parazaider on woodwinds and Danny Seraphine on drums. Each Chicago member contributes his own specialized background. Chicago-born Terry Kath experimented with the banjo, accordion, bass and drums before settling on the guitar. Terry and Walter Parazaider

McMahon Stadium, Calgary - 1974

first got together in a group called Jimmy and the Gentlemen. They later joined another band and Terry got back to playing bass. With the formation of Chicago four years later, Kath returned to guitar...

One of the greatest rewards in putting this book together has been my rediscovery of the musicians and their music. And none more than Terry Kath. Even though I met him, saw him play and shot pictures of him during two separate concerts, his brilliance didn't impact me then nearly as much as it does now. But I think that's exactly what Chicago intended. Their mission from the beginning was to be a rock'n'roll band with horns, where all the musicians were equal, with egos kept in check. It worked. Chicago became a bonafide supergroup in the early seventies, without a 'frontman' and without ever putting their faces on an album cover. The original members were together for ten years (until Terry's death) through twelve albums and countless tours. But as successful as their mission was, it also left Terry Kath the most underrated guitar player in rock'n'roll history.

In researching Terry, listening to every song and watching every bit of footage I could find, I soon realized that he was the driving force of the band. It started with *Introduction*, the first song on their first album, written and sung by Terry. The album also showcased Terry's transcendent guitar work, especially on *Poem 58, I'm a Man, Liberation* and his seven-minute experimental improvisation, *Free Form Guitar*. It's no wonder that after Jimi Hendrix saw Chicago play, he told Walter Parazaider "Your guitar player is better than me," and then had them open for him during his 1969 U.S. tour. In a 1971 Guitar Magazine interview, I wasn't surprised to read that Terry idolized Hendrix, or that he was influenced by Mike Bloomfield's playing on The Paul Butterfield Band's *East-West*.

In addition to his unequaled guitar chops, Kath was a prolific songwriter and strong lead singer. It was Terry's soulful vocals on the James Pankow-penned *Make Me Smile* that gave Chicago their first Top 10 hit, and again on *Colour My World,* both from their break-out album *Chicago II*.

Less than four year after I photographed Terry Kath, his love of guns combined with his use of alcohol resulted in tragedy. He was partying at a roadie's house in Woodland Hills and was cleaning his gun. When the roadie told him to be careful, Terry replied, "Don't worry, it's not loaded" then held the gun to his head and pulled the trigger, not realizing a round was still in the chamber.

I am thankful for the legacy Terry Kath left behind, but my newfound deeper admiration for him has left me playing a painful and pointless game of 'If only...' If only he hadn't made that stupid mistake. If only I could have seen him play in a straight-up rock band. If only he'd finished his solo album. If only we could have more of Terry Kath.

Maurice Gibb

December 22, 1949 - January 12, 2003
Intestinal Blockage

Q.E. Theater, Vancouver - August, 1974

I don't know how I would have navigated my awkward early teen years without the brothers Gibb. Even though I had a big mouth, I was painfully shy when it came relating to boys and expressing my feelings. I had no clue how the boy-girl thing worked. I still don't. But the Bee Gees were always there for me. At those teen dances that I loved and hated, slow dancing with some guy when the boy I wanted to dance with was holding someone else, *To Love Somebody* and *Holiday* made everything alright. I listened to Bee Gees - *Words, I Started a Joke, I've Gotta Get a Message to You* - the first time I went steady, when I didn't even know what going steady meant. They kept me company with *Lonely Days* when I felt like I didn't fit in and let me know it was okay to feel with *How Can You Mend a Broken Heart.*

I thought a lot about those days as I made my way to the theater for the Bee Gees show. It was always a little scary shooting and meeting a band I already had an intimate relationship with, even if it was one-sided. What if they were egotistical jerks like some of the other musicians I'd met? My all-important teenage memories would be instantly destroyed. It wasn't the first time the Bee Gees held my well-being in the balance. As I took the picture of the fans filing in to their seats I had a knot in my stomach, realizing that I was probably anticipating this night more than anyone else. I was thankful the Bee Gees were experiencing a dip in their career so I could see them in the intimate 3000-seat Q.E. Theater instead of the 17,500 Coliseum they would have played in years past or future.

Tom Kennedy (road manager), Robin Gibb, Hugh Gibb (the boys' dad), Linda Gibb (Barry's wife), Barry Gibb, Maurice Gibb

My hopes were not dashed. They were exceeded. Tenfold. The music portion of the night did not disappoint, and backstage? Well, the brothers were very sweet, and funny - especially Maurice. He had a ton of personality and really cracked me up. I was just the girl with the camera but they made me feel like part of the family. It was no surprise when they invited me to tag along for part two of the backstage party at their hotel. I was happy to soak up their presence into the night, of course, never letting on about our time together in the past. As the party wound down, I got a sweet offer from one of the brothers. Although I was tempted, I declined. I knew those things didn't last and I couldn't chance changing the profound effect they'd had on me all those years.

The Bee Gees with promoter Bruce Davidson (below left) and his assistant, Brian.

By the following year, the Bee Gees were back on top with *Jive Talkin'* and hit superstar status in 1977 with the soundtrack album for *Saturday Night Fever*. They rode the top of the disco wave through the seventies with six #1 singles including *How Deep Is Your Love, Stayin' Alive* and *Tragedy*, but then the backlash from the death of disco kept them off the charts for several years. In 1987, they bounced back with *You Win Again*, which topped the UK charts, but they failed to crack the Top 10 in the U.S. until *One* in 1989. Their thirty-plus years as the Bee Gees put them in the top ten of all-time bestselling music artists. They earned seven Grammys including a Lifetime Achievement and Legend Award, and were inducted into the Rock and Roll Hall of Fame in 1997. After Maurice's sudden death, Robin and Barry chose to retire the Bee Gees name.

Marc Bolan

September 30, 1947 - September 16, 1977
Car Crash

PNE Coliseum, Vancouver - October 21, 1974

Bolan was born Mark Feld in Hackney, London. He had his first band by the age of twelve and was driven toward stardom when their lead singer found early success with a solo career. Marc left school at fifteen to pursue a modeling and acting career but soon returned to music, making several failed recordings under the name Toby Tyler. In 1965 he signed with Decca and recorded his first single *The Wizard* using a new name, Marc Bolan. The record failed to chart but Bolan was still bent on becoming a star and managed to convince record producer/manager Simon Napier-Bell to give him a shot. After a short stint in the band John's Children, where he was noticed for his composition *Desdemona*, Marc formed Tyrannosaurus Rex with a friend, percussionist Steve Took. They toured and recorded as an acoustic duo, finding moderate success with the single *Debora*, partly due to the continued support of Radio 1 DJ John Peel.

Took was replaced by Mickey Finn after a falling out with Marc in 1969, then Bolan went electric with the addition of Steve Currie on bass and Bill Legend on drums. They shortened the name to T. Rex and Marc finally got his first hit, *Ride A White Swan*, in early '71. The hits kept coming and Bolan's dream of stardom culminated when the media dubbed the band T. Rextasy, and their March 1972 Wembley concert was made into the Ringo Starr-directed film *Born To Boogie*.

I wasn't at the Coliseum on October 21st for T. Rex. I was there to shoot Blue Oyster Cult for Columbia rep Frank Gigliotti, and was in the middle of taking pictures backstage when T. Rex hit the stage. Bolan may not have even had a record deal at the time, as this was the period his career was taking a downward turn. I didn't care. I couldn't resist sneaking off to capture a few frames of the always-magnetic Marc Bolan. It may not have been considered one of his better shows - Vancouver's Georgia Straight music paper gave them a scathing review under the headline "TWrecks" - but I will always remember the concert from my pictures, where there's no doubt Marc performed for my camera in true rock star fashion.

Bolan's career was on an upswing in 1977, with the success of his six-part hit television series *Marc* and the formation of a new band. Sadly, his resurgence was cut short when on the way home from a London club his girlfriend, Gloria Jones, lost control of their car and hit a tree, killing Marc instantly. But thirty years after his death, Marc Bolan's star continues to shine, with his official fan club boasting a membership of nearly two thousand devoted fans. He is credited with inventing Glam rock and heavily influencing the punk rock movement. There have been over twenty-five posthumous albums released and his songs have been featured in over thirty movies, from *The Truman Show* to *Billy Elliot* and *Moulin Rouge!* to *Jarhead*

Steve Currie

May 19, 1947 - April 28, 1981
Car Crash

PNE Coliseum, Vancouver - October 21, 1974

Steve Currie was born in Grimsby, North East Lincolnshire, England. After a time as a shipping clerk on the docks, he joined a local jazz rock band, then answered a newspaper ad for a bass player. It was for Marc Bolan's T. Rex. He played with Bolan from the Fall of 1970, beginning with the single *Ride A White Swan,* through several songs on *Dandy In The Underworld,* which was released in 1977. After parting ways with T. Rex, Currie worked as a session player until he was killed in a single vehicle crash near his home at Val Da Parra in Portugal.

George Harrison

February 24, 1943 - November 29, 2001
Cancer

Above: Friar Park at Henley-on-Thames, UK - May 23, 1977   *Right: PNE Coliseum, Vancouver - November 2, 1974*

I had the privilege to shoot George Harrison on the opening night of his *Dark Horse* tour. I thought it was a great show, even though a lot of people weren't happy with the Indian music that opened the concert and then became part of the encore. As I remember there was a lot of chaos surrounding the show, which was not unusual for a big production with a lot of people involved. And being the first show, I'm sure they had their share of kinks to work out.

But none of that affected me. I couldn't have been in a better mood. I was thrilled for the opportunity to take pictures of a former Beatle, and excited that I was leaving on my exploratory trip to Los Angeles a few days later. Of course, I didn't realize at the time that I would get to shoot my second former Beatle the following week, when I attended a press conference for Ringo Starr at Capitol records the very day I arrived in L.A.

The Dark Horse tour went on to have more than its share of problems, not the least of which was George's voice. He had a bout of laryngitis while trying to rush the recording of his *Dark Horse* album (later dubbed "Dark Hoarse" by the critics) before going out on the road, and the problem continued to plague him throughout the tour.

Known as the quiet Beatle, Harrison was anything but quiet when he exploded on the post-Beatles music scene in 1970 with his first solo (triple) album, *All Things Must Pass*. It quickly topped the U.S. charts along with the single, *My Sweet*

Lord. The following year he paved the way for future multi-artist benefit concerts with *The Concert for Bangladesh* at Madison Square Garden. His band included the members of Badfinger, and additional performers including Billy Preston, Ringo Starr, Eric Clapton and Bob Dylan. The triple album hit #1 in the UK and #2 in the U.S. and won a Grammy for Album of the Year in 1973. He followed with *Life in the Material World,* his third consecutive #1 release.

In 1979 Harrison formed his film production company Handmade Films. They initially provided financial backing for *Monty Python's Life of Brian,* but went on to produce a slate of acclaimed films, including *Time Bandits, The Missionary, Mona Lisa* and *Withnail and I.*

Following the murder of John Lennon, George wrote a tribute song, *All Those Years Ago,* with guest appearances by both McCartney and Starr. After a five-year hiatus from recording, George came back with the Top 10 album *Cloud Nine* and a #1 single with a cover of the Rudy Clark song, *Got My Mind Set On You.*

In 1988 the Traveling Wilburys were formed by Harrison along with Bob Dylan, Jeff Lynne, Roy Orbison and Tom Petty when George needed a B-side for a UK single he had recorded. The record company loved the song, *Handle with Care,* and asked for a Wilburys album. They ended up recording *The Traveling Wilburys Vol. 1,* which peaked at #3 on the U.S. charts and won a Grammy for Best Performance by a Duo or Group in 1990. A second album, *The Traveling Wilburys Vol. 3* was released in 1990 without Orbison, who had died suddenly in late 1988.

After surviving a bout with cancer in the late nineties, George suffered multiple stab wounds while fending off an attacker in his home in 1999, which may have resulted in a recurrence of his cancer in 2001, this time taking his life.

George Harrison, Robben Ford, Jim Horn

I didn't get to know George on a personal level but I did get to hang out at his house on two separate occasions. Without a doubt, it is the most amazing piece of real estate I have ever set foot on.

The purpose of my visit was to photograph the knobs adorning George's recording studio doors that were designed by Klaus Voormann and appeared in my *Starart* book. Before I went to England, Klaus gave me the number of a person to call that would help me get access to Friar Park, but even with the connection it was going to be difficult to arrange.

Luckily, I had already become friends with Maureen Starkey. When I told her I needed to go to George's house, she immediately picked up the phone and made a call. And just like that, we were driving through the gates of Friar Park.

We took her three kids with us and made an afternoon of it. Kumar Shankar (Ravi's nephew) lived there at the time and was our host for the day. He was really accommodating. The inside of the house was as amazing as the outside. I didn't take pictures inside, other than the doorknobs. That would have been too weird under the circumstances.

Besides, it was a beautiful day and we wanted to take advantage of it. We spent the afternoon exploring the gardens. I got the grand tour from Maureen and Kumar, along with their commentary on the history of the former friary.

They told me that when George bought the house he didn't even know the gardens were there. Everything was completely overgrown. As he was renovating, they uncovered a maze of trails, caves, and underground tunnels that led up to the house. George was meticulous in refurbishing the gardens to their original condition.

Billy Preston

September 2, 1946 – June 6, 2006
Complications of Malignant Hypertension

PNE Coliseum, Vancouver - November 2, 1974

Billy Preston was a child prodigy. By ten he was playing keyboards for gospel singers Mahalia Jackson and James Cleveland. At twelve he was portraying a young W.C. Hardy to Nat King Cole's grown Hardy in the biopic *St. Louis Blues*. As a teen he played with Ray Charles and Little Richard, and had his first record released by the age of twenty.

He was famous for playing with the biggest names in the music business, including the Beatles, the Rolling Stones, Elton John, Eric Clapton, Bob Dylan, Sam Cooke, Sammy Davis Jr., Sly Stone, Aretha Franklin, the Jackson 5, Quincy Jones, and the Red Hot Chili Peppers. He was the only non-Beatle musician to receive credit on a Beatles record for the single *Get Back*. Not content to remain a sideman, Preston signed with Apple Records and released *That's The Way God Planned It* in 1969. In 1971, his last record for Apple garnered a Grammy for his instrumental *Outa-Space*. He moved to A&M Records in '72 and had his first #1 hit with *Will It Go Round In Circles*, followed by *Space Race* charting at #4, and another #1 with *Nothing From Nothing* from his 1974 album *The Kids and Me*. That album also debuted his co-written song *You Are So Beautiful* which became a huge hit for Joe Cocker. He remained close with George Harrison after The Beatles break-up, playing on several of his solo albums and concerts, including *Concert For Bangladesh* and his *Dark Horse* tour where I shot these pictures.

Preston was not as fortunate in the eighties. His struggle with alcohol and cocaine addictions led to an arrest and conviction for insurance fraud after setting his own house on fire. Fortunately, he got his problems under control and was back on the road in 1991 with Eric Clapton, as well as touring with Ringo Starr and His All-Starr Band.

Billy Preston was plagued with health issues in his later years. He received a kidney transplant in 2002 but that wasn't enough to save him. He fell into a coma on November 21, 2005 and never awoke.

Alex Harvey

February 5, 1935 - February 4, 1982
Heart Attack

Whiskey-A-Go-Go, Los Angeles - November, 1974

The Sensational Alex Harvey Band (l to r): Hugh McKenna, Chris Glen, Zal Cleminson, Alex Harvey, Ted McKenna, Vicky Silva

You gotta wonder about a guy who names his band after himself and then puts the word 'sensational' in front of it. Who would have the balls to do that? I guess a raucous Scotsman who called himself 'The Last of the Teenage Idols' after winning a 'Scotland's answer to Tommy Steele' contest in the mid-fifties. By that time, he'd already played with several Dixieland, jazz and skiffle groups. In 1959, Harvey formed Alex Harvey's Big Soul Band, recording a couple of albums in the early sixties to moderate regional success and backing American stars touring the UK, including Eddie Cochran, Gene Vincent and John Lee Hooker. Alex Harvey was also an original band member in the London production of *Hair*. The Sensational Alex Harvey Band was born in 1972 when Harvey teamed with Zal Cleminson, Hugh McKenna, Chris Glen and Ted McKenna, all members of the band Tear Gas.

I originally thought I shot The Sensational Alex Harvey Band at the Troubadour in '75 or '76, after I moved to Los Angeles. Then I found an old list of musicians I'd taken pictures of and where I shot them but with no dates. The Whiskey was listed as the location, which made total sense because the band photos were taken from above and the Troubadour didn't have a balcony. But when did I shoot them? I couldn't find any evidence of them playing in the U.S. after 1974. Only some

December dates from when a live album was recorded, but still nothing from the Whiskey. Then it dawned on me. I shot them at the Whiskey when I came to Los Angeles on my November '74 scouting trip, which explains why the slide mounts were from the lab I used in Vancouver.

My memory on the dates and location may have been sketchy but the show Alex Harvey put on that night has been emblazoned in my mind ever since. Alex Harvey was no liar. The band was indeed sensational.

The show began with Harvey in front of a microphone, opening a large storybook. He must have looked around the audience for a good minute before he opened his mouth and said, in his lovely Scottish accent, "Good evening, boys and girls."

Alex Harvey told and sang his stories through several characters. The trenchcoat wearing detective trying to solve the case of *The Man in the Jar*, Vambo with his spraypaint can and his Brandoesque leather clad biker of *Framed* who smashed through the faux brick wall where Vambo had left his mark, VAMBO ROOLS.

I'd never seen anything like it. It was definitely rock and roll, but with the flavor of musical theater and a sprinkle of vaudeville. It was a really great show.

I've read that he wore the same striped shirt for every show. Originally it was white and black stripes, until it was washed with something that bled red, turning the white stripes to the pinkish orange in my photos.

I never would have guessed that Alex Harvey was almost forty years old when I shot the show at the Whiskey. Harvey went into semi-retirement in 1977 due to recurring back problems. Alex was on a short European tour when, two days before his 47th birthday, he suffered a massive heart attack while waiting for a ferry in Belgium.

Tammy Wynette

May 5, 1942 - April 6, 1998
Heart Failure

Tammy with George Jones, Q.E. Theater, Vancouver - November, 1974

Tammy Wynette was born Virginia Wynette Pugh in Itawamba County, Mississippi. After Tammy's father died of a brain tumor when she was nine months old, her mother found a job in Memphis, leaving Tammy to be raised by her grandparents. She had a hard childhood picking cotton but she also studied music and dreamed of being a star like her idols Patsy Cline, Hank Williams and future husband, George Jones. Tammy sang in a gospel trio during high school and was also an all-star basketball player. In 1959, a few months prior to graduation, she married her first husband. She worked as a waitress, receptionist, barmaid and in a shoe factory before earning her cosmetology license to become a hairdresser. Tammy left her husband before the birth of her third child and in 1966, with kids in tow, moved to Nashville in hopes of getting a recording contract.

After several rejections, she signed with Epic, changed her name to Tammy Wynette and soon became known as "the first lady of country." She had six #1 hits by 1970 including *I Don't Want To Play House, D-I-V-O-R-C-E* and her signature song *Stand By Your Man,* which was a cross-over hit on the pop charts. She won Grammys in 1967 and 1969 for Best Female Country Vocal Performance and claimed the first ever gold record earned by a female country star.

After a second failed marriage she married George Jones in 1969. Their tumultuous relationship ended in 1975, but they continued to record together through the mid-nineties. During the eighties and nineties, Tammy was plagued with health problems, undergoing many surgeries followed by an addiction to pain killers. The 1981 TV movie *Stand By Your Man,* starring Annette O'Toole and Tim McIntire, was adapted from her autobiography. Tammy Wynette's songs have been featured in numerous movies including *Thelma & Louise, GoldenEye* and *Brokeback Mountain.*

Papa John Creach

May 8, 1917 - February 22, 1994
Heart Failure

Commodore, Vancouver - December 5, 1974

I fell in love with Papa John Creach instantly. There was just something about him... a strong presence, yet a certain grace. Quiet and centered. He made me feel calm. Of course, on stage was a different story. At the age of 57, he rocked out with the joy of a little kid.

When I asked him if he'd mind me shooting him in his dressing room he welcomed me in and asked if there was something in particular I wanted him to do. I said, "Just pretend I'm not here." If there was a record company guy there, I didn't shoot him. My camera was trained on Papa. Every move he made was a picture begging to be captured. I loved the expression in his long thin hands. He even put artistry into the simple task of lighting a cigarette.

John Henry Creach was born into a musical family in Beaver Falls, Pennsylvania. He started playing violin as a child because his uncle had one around the house and he liked it. When he was eighteen, his family moved to Chicago so he could continue his music studies. He was a guest artist with the Illinois Symphony Orchestra and then moved into jazz and rhythm and blues. He formed the Johnny Creach Trio and played the hotel circuit, clubs and sea cruises from Los Angeles to Catalina through most of the sixties. Then one day he was standing outside the musicians union checking the gig board and struck up a conversation with a young drummer and they became friends. The drummer was Joey Covington, who went on to join Jefferson Airplane. He invited Papa John to sit in on a recording session with them; the band loved Papa and just like that the fifty-something fiddler became a rock star. He stayed with the Airplane, then played with Hot Tuna and back with the transformed Jefferson Starship. He also toured solo and recorded ten of his own albums.

Downchild Blues Band

Jane Vasey   Tony Flaim

Zodiac, Vancouver - January, 1975

Back Row: Dave Woodward, Bill Bryans, Jim Milne
Center Row: John Cordina (soundman), Jane Vasey, Nat Abrahams
Front Row: Monica Netupsky (record rep), Donnie Walsh, Tony Flaim

Downchild Blues Band was formed by Donnie "Mr. Downchild" Walsh in 1969 and has remained a mainstay on the Canadian music scene ever since. They got their start at Grossman's Tavern in Toronto, then launched their recording career the hard way. In 1971, Walsh put up his own money to record and press 500 copies of the album *Bootleg.* Sam's record store on Yonge Street fulfilled a promise to display the record in the front window. They also sold the record at their gigs and it soon came to the attention of RCA, who gave them $2000 to put it out on their label in Canada and Japan.

The band started touring back and forth across Canada and to date have played more than 7500 shows with over 100 musicians passing through the band. I was brought in to shoot them at the Zodiac club in Vancouver by my client and friend, Monica Netupsky. She worked for a company that distributed records in Canada for the smaller labels around the world. Shooting in clubs was always difficult. There's not enough room to move around and the lighting always sucks. Always. Which made it difficult for me because I would never shoot a live show with a flash. That's sacrilege.

Jane Vasey

1949 – July 7, 1982
Leukemia

Zodiac, Vancouver - January, 1975

I've always remembered shooting Jane Vasey because it was rare to find a petite beautiful blonde pounding the ivories in a rocking blues band. Physically, she was one of those girls you'd expect to see in figure skating competition; not getting down with a bunch of guys. But without a doubt, she held her own on the stage and then some.

Vasey began playing piano at the age of six and continued her classical studies until she graduated from the University of Manitoba in Winnipeg with a Masters Degree in Music and a BA in the Arts. After moving to Toronto in 1970, she spent three years playing for ballet classes and various theater productions, as well as teaching. She developed her love for the blues when a girlfriend gave her an Otis Spann record. Jane found that the blues involved the great runs and phrases that she knew from classical music.

Jane joined the Downchild Blues Band in 1973, around the time when *Flip, Flop and Fly* was becoming a hit, and stayed for the remaining nine years of her life. She was diagnosed with leukemia in the latter part of the seventies but continued her grueling tour schedule with the band in between treatments. She was known to skip a treatment to make a gig, even though the consequence was complete exhaustion. The only change she made toward the end was to fly to the next show instead of traveling in the band's van. After her death, Jane's parents set up a music scholarship in her name at the University of Manitoba in Brandon.

Tony Flaim

1948 - March 10, 2000
Apparent Heart Attack

Zodiac, Vancouver - January, 1975

Jane Vasey, Jim Milne, Tony Flaim, Bill Bryans, Donnie Walsh, Dave Woodward, Nat Abrahams

Initially I thought I'd shot the Downchild Blues Band when I first started taking pictures in Toronto. I had only glanced at the color slides and the club reminded me of a place I'd done one of my first paid shoots. I started looking up the band and saw that they had been playing around Toronto while I was there and made the assumption that I'd shot them there. That assumption led to another when I decided these pictures must be of Donnie Walsh's brother Hock, who was the lead singer at that time, not Tony Flaim.

My incorrect assumptions quickly unraveled after I sent the pictures to Donnie Walsh to identify the remaining band members. I had also looked back through my sporadic journals and figured out that I shot them in Vancouver much later, when Tony Flaim was their lead singer. Tony replaced Hock Walsh in 1974 and continued on and off with the band through 1989, sometimes even alternating with Hock.

In researching Tony, I soon realized I wasn't the only one who had made the wrong assumption. When Richard "Hock" Walsh died of a heart attack on New Year's Eve in 1999, a local television station ran footage of the band with Tony Flaim at the mic and identified him as Hock. Tony saw the broadcast, and it was later rumored that he took it as a bad omen. As it turned out, Tony considered it a stupid mistake and was only annoyed with the numerous calls he got from people wondering if he was okay. Then, sadly, less than four months later, Tony also passed away from a heart attack.

Unlike Jane Vasey, Flaim was exactly the guy you'd expect to see in front of a raucous blues band. He was an energetic performer with a big gravelly voice, clapping his hands and engaging the crowd.

Peter Bardens

June 19, 1945 - January 22, 2002
Lung Cancer

Agridome, Vancouver - February, 1975

I always got on really well with bands from England. It was probably my affinity to their sense of humor and the fact that they liked to have a good time. And Peter Bardens was no exception. At the time I met him, I had no idea of his extensive background in music industry. Maybe the English guys are modest too. He may be best known as the driving force and keyboard player for progressive rock band Camel from 1971-78, but he also had an impressive career in the sixties.

In 1964 he knocked on a neighbor's door where he heard drumming and asked the guy if he wanted a gig. The drummer was Mick Fleetwood and he credits Bardens for getting him into the music business. They formed the Cheynes and released a couple of singles before Peter was recruited to play with Van Morrison's band Them on the *Baby, Please Don't Go/Gloria* hit record. He then put together Peter B's Looners, with Fleetwood back on drums, Dave Ambrose on bass and his new discovery, Peter Green on guitar. Bardens later changed their name to Shotgun Express when he added a couple of singers, including a then unknown Rod Stewart. The group split up in 1967 after Bardens fired Stewart, and Peter Green and Fleetwood left to join John Mayall's Bluesbreakers.

After leaving Camel, he played again with Van Morrison then started the band Keats, releasing one album in '84. He moved to Malibu, California in 1985 and went on to release several solo albums, including the well-received *Seen One Light* and the follow-up *Speed Of Light*, featuring longtime friend Fleetwood on several tracks. Peter Bardens never became a huge star in name but he was always regarded as one of the best keyboard players around.

Waylon Jennings

June 15, 1937 - February 13, 2002
Diabetes

Q.E. Theater, Vancouver - March, 1975

My camera loved Waylon Jennings and I loved shooting him. We had a connection when he was onstage and it continued into his dressing room. Maybe it was the fact that he was the original country outlaw. Like most girls drawn to the music scene, I had an attraction to the bad boys. I don't think I could have taken a bad picture of him if I tried.

Waylon taught himself to play guitar by the time he was eight and had his first band at twelve. He was mentored by Buddy Holly after meeting him while working at a radio station in Lubbock, Texas in 1954. Holly produced his first single *Jole Blon* and Waylon played bass for Holly on his last tour. He was supposed to be on the fateful plane that took Holly's life but gave his seat up at the last minute to the ailing Big Bopper. The tragedy weighed heavily on Waylon for many years.

After developing his sound at a club in Phoenix, Arizona, Waylon landed a short-lived contract with A&M in Los Angeles. He then signed with RCA and moved to Nashville in 1965, where he recorded with Chet Atkins and lived with Johnny Cash. He had a string of moderate hits using the Nashville session men until the early seventies, when he began a collaboration with songwriter Kris Kristofferson that resulted in two albums including *Ladies Love Outlaws*, and later with Willie Nelson recording the classic *Mammas Don't Let Your Babies Grow Up To Be Cowboys*. His hard-edged sound and rebel attitude made him the first rock star of country. The first to say to hell with the Nashville hierarchy. The first of the outlaw cowboys.

Jennings hit it big in 1974 with two #1 singles, *This Time* and *I'm a Ramblin' Man,* and continued his ride through the seventies, amassing ten #1 hits, two Grammys and four Country Music Awards. His career then took a downward turn due to substance abuse, but he managed to beat his addiction by 1984. During his five decades in the music business Jennings recorded sixty albums and was the first country singer to sell a million records. He went on to become the narrator on *The Dukes of Hazzard* television series and contributed the theme song *Good Ol' Boys*. He also played himself in two episodes of *Family Guy*. He acted in two films, *Sesame Street Presents: Follow That Bird* and *Maverick,* and his songs have been used in over fifteen movies, including *Moscow on the Hudson, White Palace* and *Talladega Nights: The Ballad of Ricky Bobby*. Waylon Jennings was elected to the Country Music Hall of Fame in 2001, shortly before his death.

Peter Wood

April 9, 1950 - September 18, 1994
Alcohol Related Fall

Gardens, Vancouver - March, 1975

Was there a time when everyone in England named their sons Peter? Or did I just meet all of them? There was Peter Bardens, Peter Grant and one of the Deep Purple roadies I hung out with at the Continental Hyatt House was named Peter. Oh, and I knew Peter Asher when I was working on the art book. And there are three in this story alone. All English, all named Peter, and in the passage of time it seems some of them got lost in the recesses of my mind.

After I made the initial list of musicians I knew would be in this book, I decided to go through all my slides and negatives. Not that I wanted any of them to be dead but, if they were, I wanted to honor them no matter how well-known they were. It was an arduous process. I shot hundreds of bands, which meant weeks on the internet searching various sites, trying to figure who played in what band when and if they were still amongst the living.

By the time I got to the Al Stewart neg sheets, I was on autopilot. I glanced at the first sheet, saw a backstage band picture and scanned it while I looked Al up online. I found his website, confirmed he was alive, and then clicked on his "alumni" link. I immediately recognized two names; Tim Renwick and Peter White. Drawn to the name Peter, I clicked on the link to his website. Turns out he lived nearby. Without thinking I sent Peter an email with the backstage band photo that I barely looked at, telling him about the book and checking in to make sure everybody was alive and well.

Left and above: Dueling photographers. I shot Peter while Peter shot me.

Within hours, I was happily reading his return email as he identified everyone in the picture. But then I read, "Behind him is Peter Wood (piano) who died of alcohol related causes some 10 years ago. No one knows if it was a suicide or whether he just plain drank too much, despondent over a break-up with his girlfriend." I read the name again. Peter Wood. A sinking feeling came over me. I took a closer look at the band picture. Oh my God. I *knew* Peter Wood. I grabbed the Al Stewart negs and began scanning them, quickly realizing I had an inordinate number of backstage shots. The horizontal shot of me taking a photo really threw me until I saw the vertical picture of Peter and realized we were shooting each other. I completely forgot I was shooting with two cameras by that time.

My head was spinning as I looked at picture after picture of the backstage hijinx, trying to put the pieces of the puzzle together. All these photographs of Peter Wood flirting with my camera... or was he flirting with me? That sinking feeling suddenly sank into a feeling of dread. Exactly how well did I know Peter Wood? And if I knew him *that* well, why didn't I remember? As I continued working on other sections of the book, I couldn't shake the nagging feeling that I had seen Peter Wood again. Fragments of memories would pop into my head; his personality, the fun we had backstage, the thought that he may have come back to Vancouver to see me - or was that one of the other Peters? And then out of nowhere I remembered his wife's name. Maggie. Why would I know that?

Finally, I found an answer as I was reading through my journals. *New York, 10pm Jan 1/79 ...Lazed around on Sunday then went to the New Year's party at Parsons Corner. It was a great party and ended up being much more fun than I ever expected. Ran into Peter Wood who I hadn't seen in a couple of years. He's in a good space, much better than last time. Talked to his wife a lot too and she is real nice. Peter has a new group with an album coming out in Feb on A&M. I am likely going to their place for dinner on Wed nite which would be really fun. They are nice people although I may have a few problems with Peter - he wants a little more than friendship with me which*

Back: Peter White, Marc Griffiths, Al Stewart, Peter Wood, Tim Renwick, Roger Swallow
Front: Alan Mason (Janus Records), Monica Netupsky (Record Rep), Luke O'Reilly (Manager)

More mutual admiration (above) I shoot Peter posing with a cracker and (below)
Peter catches a candid of me.

I'm not into. I know what happens to chicks who fool around with married guys... (I've always remembered that New Year's party, but not because I ran into Peter Wood. The memory I held onto all these years was meeting another Peter at the party) *...Also met Peter Frampton there. He is a much nicer person than I expected - also nicer looking than in pictures. We had a nice chat and will possibly get together when I get back to L.A.*

Besides being an incorrigible flirt (in the most lovable way) and a great photographer, Peter Wood was also an extremely talented and accomplished musician. During his stint with Al Stewart, Peter co-wrote Al's biggest hit *Year of the Cat.* In the early seventies he played with The Sutherland Brothers and Quiver. In late 1975, he joined Joey Molland's post-Badfinger band, Natural Gas. They released one album and were lauded as the next big thing after they opened for Frampton on his hugely successful *Peter Frampton Comes Alive!* tour.

In 1984, he toured with Lou Reed and played keyboards on his album *New Sensations.* Other session work included albums with Cyndi Lauper, Carly Simon and Bob Dylan to name a few. He was an original member of The Bleeding Hearts Band backing Pink Floyd on their live shows of *The Wall.*

I recently reconnected with Maggie Wood and she provided me with his birth and death dates. She also confirmed that he did not commit suicide. He died as a result of head trauma that he suffered in a drunken fall at his home. Unfortunately he was alone at the time and his body wasn't found until the following day.

I know I will never forget Peter Wood again, and at the same time I wonder if I'll ever completely remember him. While my journal answered a lot of my questions, it raised yet another mystery that remains unsolved. I wrote that I hadn't seen Peter in a couple of years, which must mean I saw him at least one other time in '76 or '77. It's my ominous sentence, "He's in a good space, much better than last time." that now haunts me. Knowing Peter, that's just the way he would have wanted this to end.

John Bonham

May 31, 1948 - September 25, 1980
Alcohol Induced Choking

PNE Coliseum, Vancouver - March 20, 1975

Led Zeppelin II was the first hard rock album I ever bought. Too young to drive, I literally ran home and threw the LP on the crappy little stereo I had in my room. With headphones on, I cranked it up and went insane. The first song was *Whole Lotta Love*. Jimmy Page's screaming guitar and Robert Plant's orgasmic wails blasted in one ear, traveled through my brain, went out the other ear and then back again. The throbbing rhythm of John Bonham's drums and John Paul Jones' bass took hold of my gut and didn't let go. I'd never heard anything like it. Not that I understood the sexuality of the song at the time, but that didn't stop Led Zeppelin from viscerally touching me "Way, way down inside." I played that album over and over again until every word and every riff was etched into my being. Little did I know I would become a rock'n'roll photographer and have the opportunity to shoot them six years later. Or would I?

I had no idea what to expect when I knocked on the door of a suite at the opulent Vancouver hotel. All I knew was I had been summoned. The door opened and I faced a man with an imposing girth and greasy black hair that strung past his collar in the back but was missing in the front. If Hell had a Santa Claus, he could have been the Devil's leading man. I needed no introduction. There was no mistaking Peter Grant, Led Zeppelin's legendary manager and captain of their ship.

With barely a hello, he ushered me into the room. We sat on opposite sides of a glass dining table, in awkward silence. I was armed with a few pictures of bands I'd shot. "Would you like to see some of my work?" I asked. Before he could answer, the phone rang and he spent several minutes reaming out whoever was on the other end. He hung up the

phone and then, as if on cue, Jimmy Page walked in the room and plopped sideways into an over-sized stuffed chair. I remained cool on the outside but inside it was, "Holy shit, I'm in a room with Jimmy Page." I'm not one to get starstruck but damn, the legend was sitting just a few feet away from me. The man whose music changed me forever.

He looked exactly like I expected. Scrawny and scruffy. It was early afternoon and I couldn't tell if he'd been up all night or just rolled out of bed. I casually nodded, said hello and he responded in kind. He didn't seem to be there for any particular reason and I wondered if it had been pre-arranged that he would drop by and check me out. But, whatever the reason, I was willing to hang in there. No way was I going to open my big mouth and jeopardize my opportunity to shoot the world's greatest rock band.

The spasmodic conversation eventually focused on what they should do after the show. They were playing Seattle the following night and Jimmy couldn't decide if he wanted to stay in Vancouver or head straight out. It seemed strange that the topic was even up for discussion being that their travel dates had probably been set for months, but I guess if you're Led Zeppelin and you own a personalized jumbo jet anything can be changed. Of course, I wanted them to stay. I already knew there was a private party planned for them after the show – there was always a party – and I didn't think the club throwing it would be too happy if the band left town. I continued to sit there on display, still unaware of my purpose and unsure what to do. Should I bust in on the conversation? Should I leave?

A couple of roadies breezed in and out and the question was put to them. What did they care; they'd be moving out with the equipment right after the show. Then John Bonham showed up and was asked his preference. He didn't seem interested in the question or the answer. He just wanted Peter to sort out something with the laundry service – I think he needed a pair of pants mended before the show. The debate finally came down to a question from Jimmy Page, "Which city has the best girls?" I decided it was time to put my two-cents in and said, "By the time you get to Seattle it will be too late to do anything. You might as well stay here. At least there will be a party." Jimmy followed with, "Will there be a lot of girls?" I answered, "Sure. There's always a lot of girls." I don't know if I had anything to do with it but they decided to stay, and more important, I was told there would be a backstage pass for me and I was cleared to shoot the concert.

The capacity-filled Coliseum was shrouded in pre-show darkness. I could feel the energy of the crowd as I parted

the side curtain and made my way into the barricaded space at the front of the stage. I had it to myself, save the three or four security guards that kept the audience at bay. The anticipation was staggering. I could feel the electricity in the air. When John Bonham's cymbals crashed into the intro of *Rock and Roll* and the scrim at the back of the stage finally lit up, spelling "LED ZEPPELIN" in flashing bulbs, the crowd erupted.

Robert Plant and Jimmy Page were front and center. Plant bare-chested with his signature cascading blond curls and tight, low-cut jeans that left nothing to my imagination, and Page wizardly clad in black pants adorned with a crescent moon and stars. John Paul Jones and John Bonham, the backbone of the band, were set slightly back. JP on bass and surrounded by keyboards, quieter in presence but equally solid in performance and Bonzo buried behind his clear amber-tinted kit with his interlocking circles prominent on his bass drum. I was all over the place; shooting from the front, the back and the sides, soaking up every second of the music as I waited for my shots. Changing between my two cameras, one loaded with Ektachrome and the other with Tri-X. Oh yeah, and intermittently compiling several minutes of 8mm footage on an old movie camera I had been playing around with.

Two-thirds of the way into the show, John Bonham was deserted by his bandmates and given center stage for his *Moby Dick* drum solo. He mesmerized over seventeen thousand fans for close to thirty minutes as he blazed with his over-sized sticks and then with his hands. I'd never seen or heard anything like it before (or since). It was thunderous yet melodic, perfectly timed, true artistry.

After an extended version of *Whole Lotta Love* and *Heartbreaker,* the band headed off-stage. I was already backstage standing near the awaiting limousines, soaking up the little time I had left in the presence of Led Zeppelin. I was next to Peter Grant, watching him bark orders at anyone who crossed his path as he tried to get his boys out of the building before the fans had a chance to realize they were gone. Then, out of nowhere, Mr. Grant suddenly grabbed my arm and thrust me into one of the long black cars... right next to Robert Plant! Within seconds, we were out of the building on the way to their hotel. Never mind that my '66 Chevy II was parked in the Coliseum parking lot – I was riding in the back of a limo with Robert Plant! I didn't care if I had to walk on broken glass in the middle of the night to get back to my car.

We tumbled out of the car in front of the hotel. Plant had taken his kimono-shirt off after the show and was only

wearing those tight jeans and a small white towel around his neck. Heads turned as we walked through the lobby and into the elevator. In addition to Peter Grant, myself, and a shirtless Robert Plant, the elevator was occupied by a couple, probably in their sixties. By looking at them I could tell they had been out to some fancy restaurant, maybe even the theater. Clearly, they had no idea who they were sharing the elevator with and made no secret of their disdain toward the sweaty, half-clad English hooligan with the long golden locks. The woman whispered something in her husband's ear and then - I swear - literally turned her nose up at Robert Plant. The snub didn't go unnoticed. Plant turned to her and laughed, "I made more money the past two-and-a-half hours than your old man makes in a year." Classic. I had to cover my mouth to muffle my laughter. Who was it that said 'the sweetest revenge is to live a better life'?

We arrived at the party and I began to wonder what happened to Jimmy Page. I wanted to know if he found his good time and was curious to see his idea of a pretty girl. I wandered through the club, chatting with people I knew until I finally came upon Jimmy. He was in the same position he had been in at the hotel earlier in the afternoon, stretched out sideways on an overstuffed chair, but this time his eyes were closed and he had a close-to-empty bottle of Jack cradled in his lap. I guess the quality of the Vancouver groupies and the debate itself turned out to be moot.

John Henry Bonham was born in Redditch, Worcestershire, about 100 miles northeast of London. He knew he wanted to play drums from the age of five, banging on pots and any containers he could get his hands on. His mum bought him a snare drum when he was ten and his dad followed with his first drum kit at fifteen. He played with several bands, including Crawling King Snakes with Robert Plant, before being recruited by Jimmy Page and Peter Grant for Led Zeppelin in July of 1968.

There are varying reports on exactly what happened the night John Bonham died – was he at the pub all evening, or the pub then the studio, before going to Jimmy Page's house? – but most agree, after a night of heavy drinking (probably vodka) he was put to bed at Page's house and found dead the following morning, after choking on his own vomit. The band essentially broke up following John Bonham's untimely death. The three remaining members have gone on to successful solo careers but nothing as mammoth as the twenty-six tours and nine albums created during their eleven-plus years as Led Zeppelin. The world of rock is certainly a sadder place without the beating of Bonzo's drums.

Stanley Turrentine

April 5, 1934 - September 12, 2000
Stroke

Oil Can Harry's, Vancouver - 1975

Stanley Turrentine was raised in a musical family in the Hill District of Pittsburgh. Following in his father's footsteps, Turrentine picked up the saxophone at age eleven. His first professional experience was in 1951 at seventeen, when he played with Lowell Fulsom's blues band featuring Ray Charles on piano. Turrentine's big break came seven years later when legendary drummer Max Roach's band broke up while on tour in Pittsburgh. Mr. Roach not only hired Stanley but also his older brother, trumpeter Tommy Turrentine.

Stanley Turrentine crossed all the boundaries of jazz, blues, and rock, giving way for his distinctive warm sound to endure five decades. After recording nearly thirty albums on Blue Note, Turrentine switched to CTI in the early seventies and had a huge hit with *Sugar*. The album not only made him a mainstream star, it also debuted the music talents of Ron Carter, Freddie Hubbard and George Benson. Turrentine released over seventy albums, including several posthumously. He suffered a stroke just prior to his closing night at the famed Blue Note jazz club in New York and passed away two days later.

The multiple images I shot of Stanley Turrentine were all done in the camera. I would place the first shot in the frame, click, then forward the film while pushing the sprocket release, shoot the next frame and repeat again if I wanted three images on one frame. Although it was hit and miss, the technique worked really well with concert photography because the background areas were generally very dark.

Hank Snow

May 9, 1914 - December 20, 1999
Natural Causes

Q.E. Theater, Vancouver - May, 1975

If it wasn't for Hank Snow, we might not have had Elvis Presley. Hank met the young singer in the early fifties and brought him on as an opening act for his show. In 1954, he convinced the Grand Ole Opry to allow Elvis to appear, and introduced him to his future manager, Colonel Tom Parker.

Snow was born into a troubled family in a small fishing village on the south shore of Nova Scotia. After his parents divorced when he was eight, Hank was forced to live with his grandmother. She refused to allow him to visit his mother and would beat him when he snuck out to see her. At twelve he became a cabin boy on the local fishing schooners and used his earnings to buy his first guitar which cost less than six dollars. By 1933, he had his own radio show in Halifax and soon began touring Eastern Canada. He made his first record in 1936 with RCA, where he stayed for the next forty-seven years and became known as "The Singing Ranger."

Snow moved to Nashville in the mid-forties and later became a staple on the Grand Ole Opry stage. His self-penned song *I'm Movin' On* became the top country song of 1950, remaining number one on the charts for a record twenty-one weeks. He made over one hundred records during his career, spanning every technology from 78s, 45s, LPs, 8-tracks and cassettes to CDs. He was elected to eight halls of fame, including the Nashville Songwriters Hall of Fame, the Canadian Music Hall of Fame, the Nova Scotia Music Hall of Fame and the Country Music Hall of Fame. At sixty-one, he became the oldest country performer to have a number hit with *Hello Love*. It is rumored that Henry Gibson's character in Robert Altman's *Nashville* was loosely based on Hank Snow.

Even though I was more of a rock/blues music fan, I loved shooting Hank Snow. He was spunky and reminded me of my years growing up in the original Canadian cow town and hanging out with the cowboys at the Calgary Stampede every summer. Not forgetting his own childhood, he created the Hank Snow Foundation for Abused Children and supported dozens of foster children around the world.

17

17

Keith Knudsen

February 18, 1948 - February 8, 2005
Chronic Pneumonia

PNE Coliseum, Vancouver - May 16, 1975

Back Row: John Hartman, Memphis Horns section, Keith Knudsen
Front Row: Pat Simmons, Tiran Porter, Jeff "Skunk" Baxter, Michael McDonald

When I moved to Vancouver my first 'real' job to support my rock'n'roll photography habit was at a record store. I didn't last long at the job. I was fired because I kept pushing the new records I liked on the customers. One of those records was the Doobie Brothers' *What Were Once Vices Are Now Habits*. It didn't matter if the customer was looking for Sinatra or Mozart, I'd pull out that Doobie Brothers album and ask, "Have you heard *Black Water?*" Then promptly toss it on the store's turntable and jack up the volume.

Drummer, singer and songwriter Keith Knudsen joined the Doobie Brothers halfway through the recording of that album, replacing Michael Hossack and co-drumming with John Hartman. Born in Le Mars, Iowa, Knudsen began drumming in eighth grade and played in his high school marching band before joining a blues band in his senior year. He moved to San Francisco in 1969, where he played in a club band, then became the drummer for the Blind Joe Mendlebaum Blues Band and also played and recorded with Lee Michaels prior to joining the Doobies.

Knudsen was in his second year with the band when I shot them, and it was the first tour with former Steely Dan keyboardist Michael McDonald, who stepped in temporarily for the ailing Tom Johnston but ended up staying. From that point on Keith Knudsen shared vocal duties, including coming out from behind the drums to sing the lead on their Sonny Boy Williamson cover of *Don't Start Me To Talkin'*. They put on a great show.

Keith continued with the Doobie Brothers through their 1982 Farewell Tour, then formed Southern Pacific with fellow Doobie John McFee and recording three country rock albums. In 1987, Knudsen convinced the former Doobies to join him for a charity concert benefiting the National Veterans Foundation, which eventually led to the reformation of the band. After Southern Pacific folded in 1993, Keith played full time with the Doobie Brothers until his untimely death.

Rick Nelson

May 8, 1940 - December 31, 1985
Plane Crash

Los Angeles - August, 1976

Born Eric Hilliard Nelson in Teaneck, New Jersey, Ricky was the adorable son and standout star of his parents' long running sitcom, *The Adventures of Ozzie and Harriet*. He was a television icon by the age of nine and a teen idol by sixteen with the debut of his musical talents, singing a cover of Fats Domino's *I'm Walkin'* on the show. The song became an instant hit and for the remaining ten-year run, the show closed every episode with a song from Ricky Nelson.

While his personal life played out on television, Rick Nelson amassed thirty Top 40 hits by 1962. One of his biggest hits was in 1961 with *Hello Mary Lou* written by Gene Pitney. In 1963, he married Kristin Harmon and their first baby, Tracy, was born. He also signed a twenty-year deal that year with Decca Records. But his light faded behind the British Invasion and he failed to have another Top 40 record until 1970. His last hit came in 1972 with the self-penned song, *Garden Party*, written in response to being booed when he refused to play his old hits at a rock'n'roll revival show at Madison Square Garden.

By the time I shot him, he was playing relatively small club venues. I had a friend at the time who was dating Rick's guitar player and she dragged me along so she wouldn't have to sit alone. I didn't mind. It was fun to see him live and hear some of the songs I grew up listening to on the radio. And he was a nice guy. Cute, a little on the shy side, but nice. I took my camera probably because I didn't know how to sit and watch a show. When it came to music, my camera was an extension of my body.

Rick Nelson, along with his band, was tragically killed when his plane crashed enroute to a play a New Year's Eve gig in Dallas, Texas. Rumors ran rampant that the crash was caused by a fire started by Rick smoking base cocaine on the plane. The NTSB later established the cause to be mechanical, probably due to a faulty cabin heater. Even though Rick had a long career, he was only forty-five at the time of his death. His twin sons, Matthew and Gunnar, continue the family music legacy with their own band, Nelson.

Lowell George

April 13, 1945 - June 29, 1979
Heart Attack

Los Angeles Forum - December 19, 1975

This was the concert that changed everything. I'd been in Los Angeles for only four months - minus the month I went home after my dad died. I was doing whatever I could to get work, which wasn't much since I was from Canada and didn't have a green card. I shot a few people here and there. An Australian band who were recording at the Record Plant. An episode of the Hudson Brothers television show. But there was no real money. I was broke all the time. I didn't have my own place. Sometimes I slept in my car. And I had a pager instead of a phone. Hoping for the big call.

Finally it came. Columbia called. They asked me to shoot Dave Mason in concert at the L.A. Forum for a live album cover. My lucky break, right? Wrong. Columbia also called ten other photographers to shoot the album cover. All clamoring to get the best spot in front of the stage. And I was out-gunned. I was the only girl and the only one shooting without a motor drive. I wouldn't use one. No way you can catch an emotional moment with a motor drive. You have to wait for it. Get into the music, get inside the musician's head and know what's coming. You can't get in that zone with a freaking motor drive. I got knocked over one too many times by those animals, said "Screw this," and left to hang out backstage.

Then somebody bolted out of a dressing room, where I happened to be standing with my cameras. "Can you come in here and take some pictures?" he asked. Suddenly, I was in the middle of a celebration in Little Feat's dressing room. They were the opening act for Mason and I'd already taken the opportunity to shoot them live, but it turned out they were signing contracts for a new record deal with their label Warner Bros., and didn't have a photographer.

What changed for me was that after this concert I decided I didn't want to be part of the throng of concert photographers. I wanted to do something special, and came up with the idea for my *Starart* book. However, I did get a photo from that night on an album. Lowell picked one of my pictures of him for the inside cover of Little Feat's 1978 live album *Waiting for Columbus,* which is considered one of the greatest live albums of all time. Thank you, Lowell.

George's first band was The Factory in 1965. He then played briefly with Frank Zappa and the Mothers of Invention in '68/'69 before forming Little Feat. George was best known for his slide guitar but was also a great singer, songwriter and producer, *Shakedown Street* for the Grateful Dead being his most renowned.

Three and a half years after I took these pictures, I was driving home from a friend's place in Topanga Canyon, not far from Lowell George's house. I was about halfway down the canyon, heading toward the Pacific Coast Highway when the shocking news came over the radio. Lowell George was dead at 34.

Little Feat's Paul Barrere, Lowell George, Richie Hayward

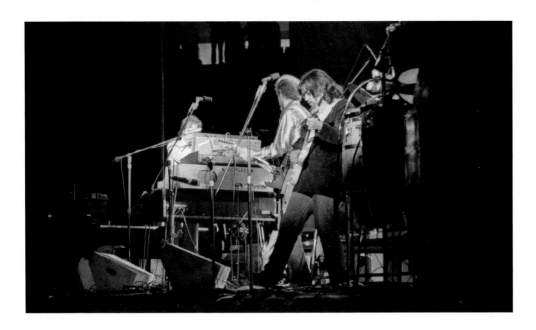

John Sebastian and Lowell George.

Mo Ostin, Lowell's son and Lowell George posing backstage at the Forum after the signing of The Big Deal with Warner Bros. Records.

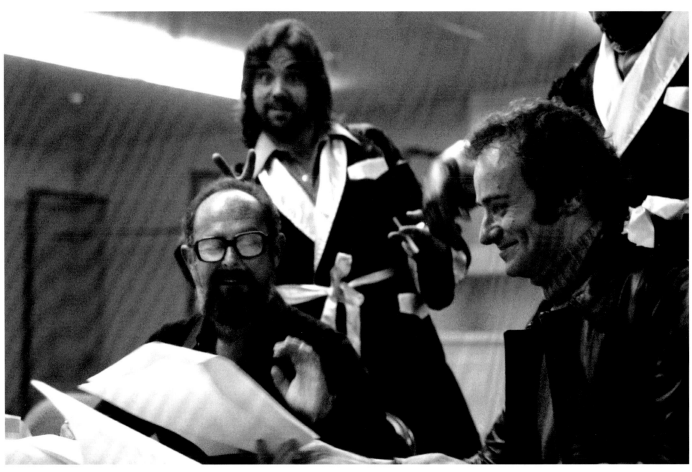

The signing of The Big Deal.

So big that Lowell didn't seem to mind the misspelling of his name.

John Fahey

February 28, 1939 - February 22, 2001
Complications from Bypass Surgery

Q.E. Theater, Vancouver - December 21, 1975

On or about December 19, 1975 I received an emergency page from Gary Switlo in Vancouver. He had booked a Christmas concert with John Fahey but Fahey was nowhere to be found. Not only was Gary selling the tickets for the show, he was the promoter. It was his show, his baby. At the time, John didn't have a booking agent, nor a manager, so I was Gary's last hope. He gave me John Fahey's home phone number and address and told me to do whatever was necessary to get him on the plane to Vancouver that evening. Seemed easy enough.

I tried calling John but there was no answer, so I got in my car and headed to Palms, a small area just west of Culver City. I lived in Hollywood and at that time anything south of Santa Monica Boulevard seemed far away. I had heard of John Fahey but was not familiar with his music or him as a person. I had no idea what to expect when I pulled up to his small, somewhat dilapidated house.

I knocked on the door and waited. And waited. I knocked again and finally heard a voice calling at me to enter. It took a minute for my eyes to adjust to the darkened living room. There was stuff everywhere. I glanced at the stacks of books, magazines, newspapers, records and the aged furniture until my eyes finally found a disheveled and cantankerous John Fahey, sunken deep into his easy chair. I introduced myself and explained why I was there. He didn't seem interested in addressing the subject of the impending show. Instead he ranted about the state of his personal life and other nonsensical musings. By the time he was done I knew much more than I cared to. Did I really need to know that he hated his neighbors

because his dogs were taken away after they accused him of abuse? I soon realized getting John Fahey on a plane was not going to be easy.

I finally steered the conversation back to the Vancouver show. How great it was going to be and how much he'd love the city. John said he couldn't go. What? "But you have to go. It's a Christmas show and the tickets are already sold out." He didn't care. I was panicking while John ran through a laundry list of excuses culminating with "I haven't slept in days" and "I don't have a road manager." I suddenly blurted out, "How about if I go with you? I'll be your road manager." What was I thinking? I don't even know this guy. And he was beyond eccentric, bordering on creepy. But I don't like to fail and there was no way I was going to disappoint Gary.

John was agreeable to the idea so I used his phone to call Gary collect and give him the update. He wasn't happy about having to spring for an extra plane ticket and hotel room because they weren't making much money on the show, but he didn't have much choice at that point. It was Friday afternoon and the concert was on Sunday. No sooner was I off the phone and feeling proud of myself when John presented me with another problem. He wouldn't be able to play if he didn't get some sleep and he'd run out of the prescription he needed. I suggested that his doctor call in the prescription and I would be happy to pick it up at the drug store. Well, that was the problem. He'd used up his allotted amount of pills for the month and his doctors wouldn't give him any more. Did I have a doctor that could get it for him? "No. I just moved here a few months ago and I don't do drugs." "Well, I can't play if I can't sleep." Shit. "I'll get it for you. What's it called and what are the symptoms they prescribe it for?"

The next thing I knew, I was sitting in the waiting room of a storefront doctor's office in East Hollywood that I pulled out of the Yellow Pages. I can't remember if it was on Normandie or Western, but it was definitely seedy. As I filled out the medical questionnaire, I worked on my spiel in my head. "I recently moved to Los Angeles and I can't sleep. I haven't had a full night's sleep in two weeks. And I can't work. When this happened before my doctor prescribed hydrochloride and it really helped. Shit. It's not hydrochloride, is it? No, no, it's chloral hydrate. Remember that – chloral hydrate... this is never going to work."

I was really nervous as I sat on the examining table, waiting for the doctor. By the time he came in I had progressed to 'jumpy.' Maybe that added authenticity to my performance. Or maybe the doctor thought I looked innocent. Either way, I walked out with a prescription for chloral hydrate. One part of me felt great. Mission accomplished. Another part of me felt sick. I was now a drug dealer. Still, I filled the prescription, packed a bag, picked up John Fahey and we were on our way to LAX. I figured out quickly what a road manager is supposed to do, at least when it's for one slightly crazy guy with a couple of acoustic guitars. Babysit.

Gary was thrilled to see me get off the plane with John Fahey in tow. Once we got John checked into his room, Gary and I had a chance to catch up. He was very excited about the show and couldn't wait to tell me about the big surprise they

Tucker in Los Angeles · May 13, 1976

had planned for John. A surprise? I'm not sure if John's the kind of guy that likes surprises. What is it? He told me they got him a special gift and it had just arrived from the Yukon. What did you get him? He said it was going to be a huge event. The press had been notified. Mark Wilson was going to play Santa Claus and present the gift at the end of the concert. What is it? A half Husky/half German shepherd puppy. Oh my God. Gary was so jazzed I didn't have the heart to tell him about John's dog issues, but I knew he needed to know.

The show went off without a hitch. John was amazing and the crowd loved him. If only they knew what it took to get him on the stage that night. We flew home the following morning. I dropped John off at his house in Palms and I went to my borrowed apartment in Hollywood. I never saw him again. Overall, it was a great trip. I turned out to be a damn good road manager. John ended up being a pretty nice guy. Oh, and I ended up with a dog.

In earlier years, Fahey started his own record company, Takoma, believing that he wouldn't be able to get a contract. In addition to finding his own success, John discovered and recorded fellow master guitarist Leo Kottke among others. But shortly after our encounter, his life and career took a downward turn. He lost his house in a divorce, developed a drinking problem and had issues with his health. He moved to Oregon in 1981 to live with his third wife. By the nineties he was living in poverty out of fleabag motels. But after a 1994 Spin magazine article spotlighted Fahey, he was re-discovered by a new generation of musicians and fans. With his resurgence, Fahey left his acoustic guitar melodies in favor of grating electronic experimentation. He opened concerts for Sonic Youth and recorded an album with Cul de Sac. In 1995, he formed Revenant Records to reissue obscure bluegrass and early blues recordings.

How Bluegrass Music Destroyed My Life, a book of his short stories and rants was published in 2000. It seems John Fahey remained irreverent to his dying day.

Malcolm Roberts

March 31, 1944 - February 7, 2003
Heart Attack

TV Studio, Los Angeles - February, 1977

I was invited to shoot Malcolm Roberts by former Tim Buckley guitarist and friend, Joe Falsia. He's the one with his hand on his forehead in the above photo. This was a rehearsal for a television variety show and, as I recall, there was some frustration on the set. I think the show's producers were hoping to turn the native Brit into an American pop idol. He definitely had the look, the accent and a beautiful singing voice, but it wasn't enough to crack the American music scene. I'm not sure what became of the variety show, if anything.

Malcolm Roberts was born in Blackley, Manchester, England and began performing in musical theater productions at age thirteen. He made his first record in 1967 on RCA but didn't break the UK Top 10 until he released *May I Have The Next Dream With You* on the Major Minor label in 1968. By the time *Love Is All* came out in 1969, he was considered one of Britain's foremost ballad singers and was also a superstar in South America. A Las Vegas gig with Jack Benny in the early seventies led to an appearance on *The Tonight Show,* but by the late seventies he moved back to England. He worked what was left of the cabaret scene in London and also returned to the stage.

In the mid-eighties he was performing on cruise ships, and spent some time in Brazil trying to attract the crowds he had in the late sixties. Later, he went back to his musical theater career in England, where he also found some success on the sixties nostalgia circuit. Even though his career had many up and downs, Malcolm Roberts maintained a loyal fan base in England and South America. At the time of his death, he was working on a new CD of original songs. It was posthumously released under the title *Rio,* in the Fall of 2003.

Gene Pitney

February 17, 1940 – April 5, 2006
Heart Failure

Larabee Studios, Los Angeles - August 3, 1977

Born in Hartford, Connecticut, Gene Pitney had his first band in high school, then gave up on a college degree in electrical engineering for a high risk career in music. His first big hit was *Town Without Pity* in 1961, which won an Oscar® for best song in the movie of the same name, and was the first popstar to perform on an Academy Awards® show. In 1962, Pitney had a Top 10 hit with *The Man Who Shot Liberty Valance*, although it wasn't actually used in the movie due to a publishing disagreement.

Gene became a big star and fan favorite in the United Kingdom, beginning with a his cover of the Jagger/Richards song *That Girl Belongs to Yesterday*, which also became the first Stones composition to chart in the U.S. Pitney later played maracas on the Rolling Stones cover of Buddy Holly's *Not Fade Away*. Other memorable Pitney hits include *Only Love Can Break a Heart, Twenty Four Hours From Tulsa* and *It Hurts to Be in Love*. While he is best known for his incredible voice, he was also an accomplished songwriter. He wrote *Hello Mary Lou* which became a huge hit for Rick Nelson in 1961, as well as the Phil Spector produced *He's a Rebel*, which topped the charts for The Crystals, and Roy Orbison's *Today's Teardrops*. Oddly enough, all the songs that were hits for Gene were written by others, while the songs he wrote only made the charts when sung by other performers.

A controversy arose over Pitney's birthdate after the Hartford Courant reported that he died at the age of sixty-six. His biography listed his birth year as 1941 but the Courant provided a birth announcement confirming that he was born in 1940. Gene Pitney passed away in his sleep at the Cardiff Hilton in the middle of a twenty-three date UK tour.

Despite his unprecedented chart success in the sixties, Pitney didn't have a #1 hit until 1989 when a duet of *Something's Gotten Hold of My Heart* with Marc Almond of Soft Cell was released in the UK. Gene was one of the few teen idols to survive the British Invasion and was finally inducted into the Rock and Roll Hall of Fame in 2002.

My day in the recording studio with Gene Pitney was a real treat. He was an ace when it came to recording; passionate and focused, yet still able to create a relaxed atmosphere. He gave me free rein to shoot whatever I wanted and even bought me lunch (that's my burger next to him on the couch). Gene Pitney was truly a sweet guy.

Harry Nilsson

June 15, 1941 - January 15, 1994
Heart Failure

Harry Nilsson, Klaus Voormann and Cynthia Webb   *Los Angeles - February, 15, 1979*

With only a ninth grade education, Harry Nilsson faked his way into a job at a California bank. The bank eventually found out he had falsified his application, but chose to keep him on. A testament to the likability of Harry Nilsson. He worked at the bank at night and wrote songs during the day. In 1960 he worked as a demo singer for $5 a song and by the time he signed with RCA in 1966, he already had songs recorded by Glen Campbell, The Monkees and The Yardbirds. His first album, *Pandemonium Shadow Show* became a favorite of The Beatles, creating a whirlwind of publicity around Nilsson. His version of Fred Neil's *Everybody's Talkin'* became a break-out hit when it was chosen for the film *Midnight Cowboy,* and his cover of the Pete Ham/Tom Evans song *Without You* from *Nilsson Schmilsson* topped the charts in '71. Nilsson created the children's animated film *The Point!* spawning another hit, *Me and My Arrow.* He also wrote the Three Dog Night hit, *One.* He managed to maintain a high profile as a singer/songwriter throughout his career even though he never performed live.

In early '74, Harry became entrenched in negative publicity after a drunken evening with John Lennon at the Troubadour, where they were ejected for heckling the Smothers Brothers. Unfortunately, he also became known for owning the infamous London flat where Mama Cass Elliot died on July 29, 1974, followed by Keith Moon on September 7, 1978. Prior to meeting Harry, I spent many a night at the flat in the Spring of '77 when I was in London to work on *Starart* with Cat Stevens and hanging out with Maureen Starkey. It was a beautiful home, with none of the bad vibes one might expect.

When I first had the idea to do this book, I thought I'd only be honoring twenty musicians. Harry was one of the twenty I knew off the top of my head. The image of him with the candle flame had always remained with me. I guess an intimate family dinner with Harry is not something you forget. But when I found the still unmounted slides tucked away in an unmarked envelope, I couldn't figure out what was going on at the table. I was living at Klaus and Cynthia's house. Klaus Voormann was in my *Starart* book and they kindly adopted me when I lost my sublet. I got as far as identifying the slides on the table. They were from my book and I had been showing them to Harry. But what was in the box Cynthia was hugging and what was that card in Harry's hand? And why were they laughing? These questions continued to eat away at me until I finally came across this journal entry: *L.A. 3pm Sat. Feb. 17/79. Thursday was pretty much of a write-off... I got myself somewhat together for the dinner party. That was really great. Cynthia made fresh baked deep sea bass and it was really good... Anyway, all the people here were great. Harry Nilsson ended up staying 'til 4am and we played $20,000 Pyramid which was incredibly funny.*

$20,000 Pyramid. Silly me. I should have remembered that's what famous musicians do after a fine meal of sea bass. I put the first ellipses in place of my boring day which included a nap and picking up Klaus and Cynthia's son, Otto. The second represents a minor rant about a girlfriend I invited to the dinner who got drunk and made a complete fool of herself. The dinner was in celebration of Harry, Klaus and their families leaving for Malta the following week to work on Robert Altman's *Popeye.*

Despite all of his success, Nilsson was in financial ruin by 1990, after an advisor embezzled most of his earnings. Following a heart attack in '93, Harry worked tirelessly to insure his family's financial security. Sadly, he died just after finishing the vocal tracks on his last album, which remains unreleased.

Acknowledgments

I could not have done this book without the help and support of others.

Thank you to all the musicians for the great times,
and the gift of their music, which kept me going every day.
Please listen to their music while you read this book.

Scott Mullen, John Chesher and Tyler Chesher
for taking the time to read my words and fix them accordingly.
The remaining mistakes are all mine.

SL Digital
Samuel Garcia, Louie Garcia, Ramon Carrazco, Mike Garcia, Hector Salazar
for taking care of the bulk of the scans and the proofing.
Special thanks to Sam for going the distance.

Digital Fusion
Christina Olsen, Hugh Milstein, Peak Scott for their fine work.

Palace Press International
Roger Ma, Marc Moore, Susan Curtin, Michael Madden, Noah Potkin
Ronald, Aubrey and Tiger on pre-press, Irene and Bevin on the press.

To the friends and families of the musicians.
Christopher Parker, Allen & Valerie Bloomfield, Beau Nilsson, Gabe Butterfield,
Salli Squitieri, Janice Switlo, Tony Zeffertt, Donnie Walsh, Erin Darlow, Peter Bell,
Maggie Wood, Tim Renwick, Peter White, Steve Chapman, Al Stewart,
Fred Kaplan, Marty Wolff, Al Kooper, Joe Falsia, Ellie Gibbins

To everyone who provided invaluable information and sources,
and to all my friends, family, blog friends and supporters.
Tom Worrall, John Ford, Monica Netupsky, Frank Gigliotti, Tom Harrison,
Dan Matovina, Jeff Johnson, Harry Funk, Dave Chamness, Paul Mercs,
Randee St. Nicholas, Jaimie Baxter, Adam Chordock, Marion Adriaensen, Sue Garvock,
Joshua Temkin, Eddy B, Brian Mathieson, Joyce Viccars, Barbara and Larry Yopyk

Very special thanks to my dad, Cecil Edmund Chesher (1918-1975), for making this book possible.